BOTTLED DEMON

FASA CORPORATION
1990

BOTTLED DEMON

Writing
James D. Long

Development
Tom Dowd

Editorial Staff
Senior Editor
Donna Ippolito
Assistant Editor
Kent Stolt

Production Staff
Art Director
Dana Knutson
Production Manager
Sam Lewis
Cover Art
John Zeleznik
Cover Design
Jeff Laubenstein
Illustration
Tim Bradstreet
Rick Harris
Joel Biske
Layout
Tara Gallagher

Printed in the United States of America

Published by
FASA Corporation
P.O. Box 6930
Chicago, IL 60680

TABLE OF CONTENTS

IRON JAWS: A PROLOGUE

Captain Grissim took one long, last drag on his nicostick and tossed the glowing butt across the empty parking lot. He watched idly as it arched briefly and skittered to a stop, sending ashes and sparks dancing across the asphalt. It was kind of pretty the way the sparks died out one by one. Grissim leaned back against the sloped hood of his Citymaster, enjoying the surprisingly clear, moonlit night. Behind him, he could hear one of his men approach. He glanced again at the pale orange glow of his dying cigarette.

"Just like tonight," he mused aloud. "Watch 'em die, one by one."

"Captain?"

Grissim absently rubbed the two-day growth of beard on his chin and neck as he turned to stare contemptuously at what his superiors referred to as an aide. From what he could tell, the guy was little more than some lop-eared techie with a datajack. Fresh out of the academy, with no more sense than some drek-headed dreamchipper. In only six short hours, Grissim had grown to despise the young Elf. How, he wondered for the hundredth time, was he supposed to make a soldier out of such rot? He rolled his eyes in a silent plea for mercy, or maybe justice.

"What is it, trooper?" he asked.

"Banes, on Tac-2, sir. His men are in position on the far side of the junk yard—"

Grissim smacked the trooper's cheek without conscious thought. Damn kids. They didn't know anything.

"Across the *what*, Trooper? Across the *what*? Why do you think we make up those cute little codes back at HQ? For the fun of it?" Grissim whacked him again, though he was sure the Elf had already realized the error of his ways.

"I thought you daisy-eaters were supposed to be tuned to all that magical mumbo jumbo. I thought you knew about magical spying. I guess I was wrong. Was I wrong, trooper?" In reality, Grissim wasn't really worried about someone overhearing his aide's mention of their target. The pair of wage mages attached to his force had given him the all-clear signal five minutes ago, and they would have noticed if someone was about to try something tricky. Still, it paid to be careful, especially because no raid on Black's Junk Yard had ever gone according to plan. Besides, the Elf had to learn sooner or later, and Grissim enjoyed this part of the training.

"S-s-sorry, sir."

"Yeah, right. Sorry. Well, if you're sorry, then it must be O.K. Think, boy. You've got to be thinking all the time. Now what is it?"

"Banes is in position. The target is quiet. The new group appears to have moved into position and seems to be waiting on their contact. They are scanning, both magically and physically, but they are not searching this far out. Both our squads are ready to move in."

"Good, trooper. That's real good. Now, back to your post. Tell the boys to saddle up. We move when I give the word."

Grissim adjusted his field jacket and watched the Elf climb into the depths of the Citymaster. Feeling the hairs rise on the back of his neck, he could tell that it wouldn't be much longer. Time for a payback, and everybody knew how painful that could be.

Grissim headed for the command couch of the Citymaster and considered his good fortune. Only eight hours ago, one of his larks had spotted his old nemesis Bloodwing leaving the Snohomish Sheraton in a rush. Among the handful of people alive who could ID the notorious Elven hitman, Bloodwing's joygirl was one and Grissim was another. The joygirl was also Grissim's lark. As luck would have it, the Captain was only a few blocks away at the time of the tip, and arrived on the scene in a matter of seconds.

It was no surprise, though, that his lark had already vanished and Bloodwing was nowhere to be seen. The hotel desk clerk was extraordinarily helpful, with a little motivation from the Ares Predator Grissim brandished under the clerk's nose. Directed to Room 616 on the sixth floor, Grissim found everything just as he had expected.

Bloodwing had been typically efficient, killing the room's three occupants with three precise shots. By the looks of them, they were "back-to-nature" Elven runners. The scene was as clean, almost sterile, as one would expect one of the town's best Elven hitmen to leave it. But under the body of the third victim, Grissim found a shattered pocket secretary. He wondered if the hitman had truly intended to kill the woman and shatter the recorder with the same bullet. It would have been a tricky shot, but the kind for which Blackwing was famous. Whatever the Elf's intent, the shot had trashed the pocket secretary. That wouldn't stop Grissim, however. A lot of people owed him some big favors.

As it turned out, he only had to cash in one favor to get a partial reconstruction of the dead Elf's last conversation. Most of it was still garbled except for the words, "Four A.M." and "Black's Junk Yard."

Snapping out of his reverie, the Captain ducked into the spacious Citymaster and leaned into the command couch. From here, he could oversee the entire operation. Strapping on the headgear with one hand, he used the other to flip a bank of toggle switches. Lights began to flash. Good. Grissim liked a lot of lights. He glanced at the amber display to his left, double-checking the Citymaster's readings. He confirmed what his rigger Ronnie already knew; everything was ready to roll. When a certain red light flashed on the console, Grissim hit the switch and listened.

"Group Two moving into position, sir. Five or six additional contacts. Total eight/nine in the net."

Grissim grinned. The terrorists with whom Bloodwing was supposed to link up had showed. Fine. He'd take them all down tonight.

"That's a roger. Keep the astral boys flying. We're on the way." Grissim keyed the open channel. "This is it, campers. Blue One, move out. Gold One, follow my lead. Ronnie, take us in."

Grissim could feel the big Citymaster roll forward as the rigger slipped into gear and pulled away from the attendant patrol cars. He glanced at the forward-mounted security camera as a side gate to Black's swung into view. He knew, no matter what happened next, that it was going to be a blast.

The Citymaster tore through the gate with a crash, immediately encountering a column of crushed cars. Without pause, Ronnie swung the beast to the right and began to charge down the narrow lane.

"Blue One, this is Leader. We are in the perimeter. Ronnie, give me ETA."

"ETA thirty seconds."

Grissim glanced at the monitor. "You heard the man. Get a move on, Blue. You're going to miss the excitement." Grissim watched several cameras as the Citymaster flew past the ancient walls of rust. His mental timer counted down the seconds as his adrenaline pumped wildly.

"Swope, take the water cannon. Hose them down good. We'll sort it out back at the station." Behind him, Grissim heard his assistant climb into the cupola, the glamour slot on the Citymaster. Though he wouldn't admit it, Grissim hoped the kid would do well. "Any grief, Swope, and hose them with lead."

Ronnie's chipped voice filled his headphone.

"ETA in ten, nine, eight. All passengers, prepare for immediate impact. Five, four. Blue reports initial contact. One. Impact!"

INTRODUCTION

Bottled Demon is a roleplaying adventure set in the world of **Shadowrun.** The year is 2050. Advances in technology are astonishing, with Humans able to blend with computers and travel through that netherworld of data known as the Matrix. Even more astonishing is the return of Magic. Elves, Dragons, Dwarfs, Orks, and Trolls have assumed their true forms, while megacorporations (rather than superpowers) rule much of the world. Moving among it all like whispers in the night are the shadowrunners. No one admits their existence, but no one else can do their secret work.

This story takes place in the streets, sewers, and shadows of the Seattle metroplex, now an urban sprawl encompassing some 1600 square miles on the eastern shore of Puget Sound. Yet even this vast megaplex is but an enclave set amid even larger states ruled by Native American nations and other sovereign states of Metahumans and Awakened Beings.

GAMEMASTER'S NOTES

Bottled Demon uses a decision-tree format, meaning that the players' team could arrive at the same encounter via various different routes, depending on choices they make during roleplay. They could also just as easily miss a planned encounter altogether. To run the adventure, the gamemaster needs a thorough familiarity with the contents of this booklet, as well as a working familiarity with the basic **Shadowrun** rules. The contents of this booklet are for the gamemaster's eyes only, except for certain items earmarked as handouts for the players. Everything needed to roleplay **Bottled Demon** is included here.

Bottled Demon is designed for a team of four to eight player characters. The group should contain a variety of talent, including one or more Magicians. At only one point in the story would a player-character Decker be needed, so a non-player character could fill his role, if necessary. Note also that combat skills are *very* important to this being a successful run.

This adventure combines several approaches. Some encounters are thoroughly planned out and described in detail. Others merely set the scene and remain open-ended. Hints for gamemastering the various situations are included with the individual sections that make up **The Adventure.**

MAKING SUCCESS TESTS

During the course of the adventure, the players will make a number of Unresisted Success Tests using a skill and a given Target Number. These Unresisted Success Tests will be indicated by the name of the appropriate skill and the target number. For example, a Stealth (4) Test refers to an Unresisted Stealth Success Test, with a Target Number 4. Sometimes it is necessary to make die rolls against a table that includes different information for different Target Numbers. If the roll is successful, the character obtains all the information for that target as well as from all lower Target Numbers.

HOW TO USE THIS BOOK

Aside from the basic **Shadowrun** rules, this book includes everything needed to play this adventure. The gamemaster should read through the entire module before beginning the game. Some important plot developments will not become apparent until well into the adventure, but the gamemaster will have to lay the groundwork much earlier on. He can only do that by being familiar with the storyline.

The gamemaster should also examine the maps, plans, and diagrams found in the adventure, especially the maps for Black's Junk Yard and Geyswain's Lair. Where appropriate, the maps are coded with letters and numbers to link an area to its description in the text.

Though this book tries to cover all the likely—and even unlikely—things that can happen during the adventure, it is impossible to foresee everything. The gamemaster may find that sometimes it is a good idea to just let the unexpected lead where it will.

The **Plot Synopsis** is a fairly detailed summary of both the story background and the course the adventure is intended to follow.

The **Adventure** begins with the section entitled **Into The Night.** Following this are a number of short sections describing each of the encounters that the players will face or are likely to face in the course of roleplaying **Bottled Demon.**

Most of the encounters begin with a text entitled **Tell It To Them Straight**. This is intended to be read, verbatim, to the shadowrunners. It describes where they are and what is happening to them as though the player characters were actually there. **Any special instructions to the gamemaster are printed in boldface type**.

Next comes the information entitled **Behind The Scenes**. This is the real story, for only the gamemaster knows what is really going on at any given moment in an adventure. If there is a map needed to play this encounter, it is included in this section. Non-player character stats needed to roleplay the section are usually included here, too.

Finally, each section includes hints entitled **Debugging**. These notes could include suggestions for getting the story back on track if things go too far wrong. For example, most gamemasters will not want the characters to get too discouraged or killed off too easily. The gamemaster is, of course, always free to ignore these hints and to let the chips fall where they may.

Legwork contains the information the player characters can obtain through their Contacts or through the public data nets.

Cast Of Characters includes pre-generated player and non-player character descriptions and stats.

Picking Up The Pieces includes tips on Awarding Karma and contains newsnet items for handout to the players, depending on the outcome of the adventure.

Playing With Darkness provides gaming information for the mysterious idol at the center of this adventure.

The news items are for handout to the players, depending on the adventure's outcome.

PLOT SYNOPSIS

Pietr Fiegeton owns and operates The Guiding Hand, a small talismonger/lore shop in the Redmond District. More popularly known as Topal, he is a small-time magician, an unassuming person in a not-so-unassuming world.

His life changes forever the day an old friend comes bursting through the door of the shop. The man appears to be scared out of his mind, deliriously mumbling strange words about a discovery he has made in the South Pacific. A battered briefcase is chained to his wrist. His health is obviously failing and he dies soon thereafter, leaving Topal to uncover the secrets of the black case.

Inside the briefcase is an ornately carved wooden box. Topal opens the box and gazes upon a talisman, a vaguely demonic-looking idol carved from deep-red stone. The object's eyes are glowing, as is the pinkish ball it clutches to its chest. Strange symbols and markings are etched into the stone. Though he cannot fully understand their meaning, Topal does sense a power in these symbols. Touching the stone, he feels tremendous energy surge through him. The world of far greater magic than he has ever known has suddenly opened up for him.

Topal cannot resist the temptation to explore the strange, new powers, but as he does, his own physical body starts to deteriorate. Then terrifying dreams begin to haunt his sleep, telling of death and darkness. Only by a supreme act of will is he able to see that this idol is too dangerous, too evil—for himself or for anyone. Meanwhile, his shop has burned to the ground as a result of his tampering with the idol. Topal finally breaks free of the object's power and puts out the word that he wants to sell it.

The shopowner is contacted by a group of Elven scholars, and a meeting is arranged. What Topal does not know is that news of this strange object has spread throughout the Elven nation of Tir Tairngire, attracting the attention of another interested buyer. This individual hires an Elven team, led by the notorious hitman Blackwing, to obtain the talisman by any means necessary.

Blackwing moves quickly, conveniently disposing of the Elven scholars before the arranged meeting. Topal has, however, taken the prudent step of hiring the team of player char-1acters as bodyguards. With them at his side, he goes to Black's Junk Yard to meet the buyers for the idol. Seeing an unfamiliar Elf instead of the one who contacted him, Topal hands the black briefcase over to a player character before stepping out into the open. Little does he realize that the strange Elf is Blackwing.

As this is going on, the forces of Lone Star Security prepare to move in. Tipped off by informants, Captain Grissim has also come to Black's Junk Yard, leading a detachment of Lone Star street cops. They want Blackwing for the murder of the Elven scholars, and as yet know nothing at all about the talisman. Grissim sees Topal and his team in the yard and immediately assumes that they are associates of Blackwing. Grissim gives the order and the troops move in. In the ensuing firefight, Topal is killed. The player characters, however, escape with the idol. Blackwing and his team also make it out alive.

Now the adventurers are in possession of something they little understand, except for knowing that at least one man has lost his life because of it. What they find out soon enough is that everyone is after them. Lone Star still thinks they are hooked up with Bloodwing. Bloodwing himself wants the idol. False rumors are circulating on the street that the team killed their employer to obtain the idol, and for such a dishonorable breach of contract any squatter or runner may be willing to turn them in. Finally, there are Topal's friends, a ragtag group of wizards known as the Children of Sophocles, who are out to avenge his death.

The first thing the team must do is find out all they can about this strange artifact. They hear of an old woman, a Dog shaman named Trixy, who has been having recurrent dreams of just such an object. They bring the idol to her. She takes one look at the symbols and knows it is evil. She tells the team that it must be destroyed, and that only a Dragon has both the power and the wisdom to do so. Trixy warns them that not every Dragon who can destroy it will actually want to. The temptation of possessing such power, she says, may be too strong. The team is told to go see the Dragon Geyswain.

Geyswain lives in a huge, arid penthouse on the top floor of the Lochlann Center, his real estate investment corporation in Tacoma. The team arrives and gives Geyswain the talisman, believing that he will destroy it. What the player characters do not know is that Geyswain is only a Dracoform who has not the power to destroy the idol, even if he wished. Indeed, he is so tempted by the object's power that he will say or do anything to possess it.

The runners are now rid of the idol, but the danger is far from over. Lone Star and Blackwing are still out there. The team's reputation remains as tainted as ever. It is then they meet Arleesh.

Arleesh is a Great Feathered Serpent, one truly possessed of immense magical abilities. Right away she tells the team that they made a grave mistake in giving the idol to Geyswain. She also insists they must help her to get the idol away from Geyswain because it is their fault he has it. The team has no choice.

Together, Arleesh and the team go back and break into the Lochlann Center. The astral plane surrounding Lochlann is teeming with spirits and elementals, while inside the building everything is quiet. Too quiet. Arleesh goes on ahead, sending the team to check out security. All the computer systems are down. All the security guards are dead. Something terrible has happened here.

After hurrying to meet Arleesh in the top-floor lair of Geyswain, they find the Dragon feeding on a corpse, his body now covered with hideous sores and weeping scars. The power of the idol has consumed him. Someone comes staggering out of the darkness. It is Bloodwing. He and his assassins trailed the players' team here the first time they came to see Geyswain at Lochlann, then they made the fatal mistake trying to seize the idol from Geyswain.

Now Lone Star reenters the picture. Following up on strange reports that Lochlann employees were not returning home after work, Captain Grissim has surrounded the building with his men. Grissim is ready to move in, but the fact that this is private property prevents him from doing so. He waits and lets the others fight it out.

With Arleesh cloaked in an Invisibility Spell, the player characters join up with Bloodwing to engage Geyswain in battle. Eventually the runners are able to seriously wound the dracoform to the point where he can no longer fight. Arleesh then reappears, snatches the mysterious idol from Geyswain's grip, and uses all her strength and power to defuse it.

Bloodwing is immediately arrested, but because he has diplomatic immunity (he shows proper identification as an Associate Ambassador from Tir Tairngire), Grissim must let him go. He takes with him the mysterious talisman and returns to his native nation. It takes some talking, but the team is finally able to clear their reputation and return safely to the shadows.

TELL IT TO THEM STRAIGHT

Here you all are, sitting around at Yoshiro's Restaurant and Bar, enjoying the finer side of a life spent running the shadows. It's only mid-afternoon, but you are already up and moving about, renewing old contacts, and generally keeping up the good will that's helped make your team so successful. It's all part of the overhead, and you know it. You've got to see and be seen in all the right places and Yoshiro's is definitely one of those.

Just as you are about to ease over to the bar, you notice a chubby man waddling toward you. It's obvious from his gait and the look in his eye that you are the ones he is seeking. He is decked out from head to foot in clothes that would be tres chic, indeed, if they weren't so much the worse for wear. Manacled to his right wrist is a black alloy briefcase. Obviously a courier's case, it seems strangely out of place with this man. He looks at you with weary, haunted eyes and speaks in a high, cracking voice.

"Thank the stars. We must talk at once. You can't know what I have had to do to find you. Let us retire to the restaurant and enjoy our midday repast. Come. Time is of the essence and there is business to discuss."

Ah, the magic word. *Business*. Grabbing your drinks, you head into the restaurant section of Yoshiro's, where your portly companion slides into a corner booth, his back to the wall. He has taken the choice seat, but so would you if he hadn't done so first.

"My name is Topal," the man says. "I require the services of several bodyguards to accompany me to a business meeting tomorrow morning. I have sought you out because of your reputation." Topal lets the praise sink in as he browses the menu. Barely seeming to give it a thought, he orders three entrees and two desserts.

"The location must, of course, remain a secret, but I can tell you it will take no more than three hours of your time, start to finish. In return for your protection, I will pay you 5,000 nuyen each. An excellent price for such a short piece of work." Topal eyes each of you in turn, looking pleased with the effect of his outrageous offer. As the waitress serves the first of his three meals, he awaits your response.

BEHIND THE SCENES

Pietr Fiegeton, or Topal, is a man in over his head. Three days ago, Simon Templeman, an old friend and fellow member of a mystical fellowship known as the Children of Sophocles, stumbled into Topal's lore shop, the Guiding Hand, with a beaten-up black alloy briefcase handcuffed to his wrist. Simon was delirious with fatigue and hunger, or so Topal thought. Despite Topal's best efforts, his friend died later that same day, wracked with pain. To his everlasting regret, Topal took possession of the briefcase.

Looking inside, he was perplexed to discover an oddly carved wooden box with a notched cover. The box opened easily. Within, resting gently in the center fold of a richly embroidered black cloth pillow, was an idol. Just over 30 centimeters long, it was carved from deep-red stone into a demon-like shape. In its hands was a pinkish globe, and its eyes glowed. Etched into the object were strange markings, whose patterns were mysterious and yet seemed to Topal almost recognizable. Almost.

What he did recognize was *power*.

The carved idol was obviously a magical item of considerable magnitude. Even stranger was the fact that Topal could use the item, though he had not personally created it. After a few minor experiments, he discovered that it would serve as a power focus to significantly augment his own magical abilities. This powerful object was now his, and no one would take it from him.

Meanwhile, the coroner attributed Templeman's death to natural causes, despite his surprise to learn that the deceased was only 42, not in his late sixties, as his physical condition suggested.

The night after Templeman's cremation, Topal tried and failed to complete a simple conjuring using the idol's power. A few hours later, the dreams began. Images of death and decay came upon him dark and menacing, but his greed for the idol's power made him heedless. Swirling around Topal, the signs told him that the carved object was dangerous, but it was only a direct personal threat that made him see the truth. He awoke to find his shop in flames.

The destruction of his shop, the terrifying dreams, and the sudden awareness that his body was deteriorating rapidly awakened Topal to the truth. He finally realized—but only by a tremendous feat of will—that he must get free of the idol.

Using his connections, Topal quickly found a group of Elven scholars interested in buying the talisman from him.

During the encounter with the players' group, Topal constantly puts one hand or the other (even though one is handcuffed to the briefcase) into the folds of his coat, where he stores a hoard of jawbreakers. These he crunches without pause. After his initial offer, Topal allows the team to set the pace of negotiations. Make an Opposed Negotiation Test. For every additional success that the team scores, Topal's final price increases by 10 percent. If Topal manages to beat the team, his initial offer stands firm. Topal agrees to pay half the money immediately and the other half upon completion of the mission. He will not tell the team where they are going or the nature of the meet. Nor will he reveal whether he is buying or selling. Once the team agrees to accept the sketchy assignment, Topal speaks, all the while bolting down the remainder of his food:

"Good, good, good," he says. "I knew I could count on you. But do not be late. That is most important. You must return here to Yoshiro's before 3:00 A.M. tonight. Bring your own transportation. I will be traveling in a separate vehicle. I am counting on you, and I need your help." Topal licks the remains of his food from his fingers, then pops another jawbreaker as he turns to leave.

The team may decide to continue relaxing at Yoshiro's, or they may want to get a little rest before the meet at 3:00 A.M.. If that is their choice, proceed to **Going To The Devils**, the next section. If the team wants to sniff out some information on their new employer, go to the **Legwork** section.

DEBUGGING

Refusing the job is about the only thing the players can do wrong here. If they do not get into the spirit of things right away, tell one of the players, preferably a magician, that he is strangely drawn to the shaman. He feels a need to help this obviously desperate man.

If that fails, Topal is willing to pay almost anything the team demands. Fatigued to the point of collapse, he has begun to fear for his life. He may not know the exact nature of the idol, but he does know it will kill him unless he can get rid of it quickly. Unfortunately for Topal, it is already too late.

TOPAL

Topal was, until recently, the sole proprietor of The Guiding Hand, a small, but profitable talismonger/lore shop in the Sophocles neighborhood of Redmond. Business was good and Topal enjoyed a good bit of prestige among the locals. His world came crashing down several days ago when an old acquaintance brought the idol into his shop.

Last night, he finally found a buyer for the mysterious item, an enclave of Elven magicians. Topal spent the remainder of the night and most of this morning calling his contacts for suggestions on muscle to accompany him. A mutual contact recommended the players' team to Topal.

Attributes	**Skills**
Body: 2	Car: 2
Quickness: 2	Conjuring: 6
Strength: 1	Etiquette (Street): 5
Charisma: 4	Firearms: 3
Intelligence: 4	Magical Theory: 6
Willpower: 4	Negotiation: 3
Essence: 6	Sorcery: 5
Magic: 6 (1*)	
Reaction: 3	

Note: *Use this rating if Topal is more than 4 meters from the idol. See **Playing With Darkness**, p. 51.

Dice Pools
- Astral: 15 (10*)
- Defense (Armed): 1
- Defense (Unarmed): 1
- Dodge: 2
- Magic: 6 (1*)

Gear
- Armor Clothing (3/0)
- Colt American L36 Light Pistol [9 (clip), 3M2]
- Mitsubishi Runabout
- Pocket Secretary
- Reusable Detection Fetish

Totem
- Raven

Spells

Combat:
- Mana Bolt: 3

Detection:
- Analyze Device: 4

Illusion:
- Entertainment: 4
- Mask: 3

CONDITION MONITOR

MENTAL PHYSICAL

Unconscious.> Possibly dead
< Unconscious. Further damage causes wounds.
Seriously > Wounded.
< Seriously Fatigued.
Moderately > Wounded.
< Moderately Fatigued.
Lightly > Wounded.
< Lightly Fatigued.

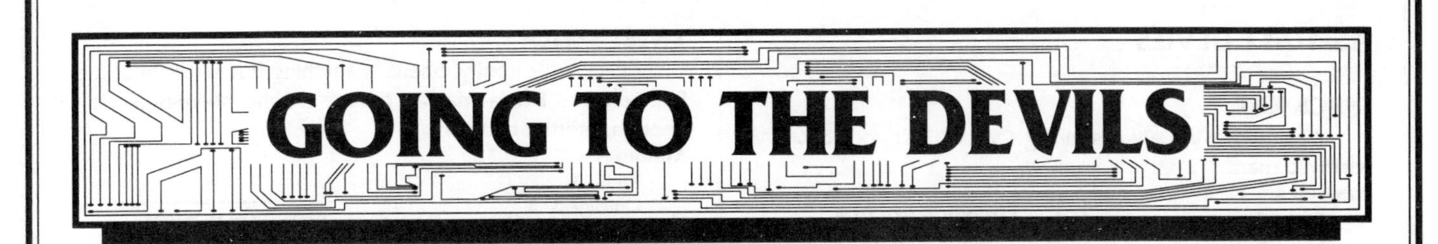

TELL IT TO THEM STRAIGHT

It is almost 3:00 A.M. As you idle your vehicles outside Yoshiro's, a cool breeze freshens your senses. It is an especially calm night, with a full moon shining down from a cloudless sky. That could be a bad omen, but then, if you played the odds, you wouldn't be in this line of work.

As an out-of-tune Mitsubishi Runabout rounds the corner, the team is bathed in halogen lights. The car slows down to pull up alongside. The lone occupant leans over, exposing his face to the street lights. In their harsh glare, the man looks ten years older than he did inside the softly lit Yoshiro's. His face is lined and wrinkled, and dark circles around his eyes give him an even more haunted look. He eyes the group nervously.

"Good, good, good. You brought plenty of weight. We shouldn't need it, but who knows? Elves can be a tricky lot. If you're ready, we'll go."

Without waiting for a reply, Topal pulls off, his groundcar slowly gaining speed. Though his path is serpentine, he is obviously en route to the Puyallup Barrens. No wonder he wanted the muscle. Most people wouldn't travel these streets in broad daylight, let alone in the middle of the night. Following him onto Jefferson, you pick up the speed, hoping to avoid the go-gangs that haunt the area.

A squeal of tires and the first cry of a chopped hog tells you your luck just ran out.

BEHIND THE SCENES

All unwittingly, Topal has led the team straight into the heart of Asphalt Devil territory. Not that it would do much good to try to avoid the Devils. It and other gangs swarm over the Barrens. It the players' group hadn't run into these gangers, they'd only have run into another bunch.

This contingent of Devils is out to protect their stretch of highway while the rest of the gang is off raiding elsewhere. Cruel and vicious, they are bored easily, especially at this time of night. If they can run the team off their territory, it would be a moral victory. If they can salvage some spare parts in the bargain, so much the better.

Go to Vehicle Combat. The conflict starts in Restricted Terrain (Normal Terrain at night), with the go-gang trailing the last vehicle in the team's convoy by 50 meters. The six go-gang members ride Rapiers and Scorpions at an initial speed of 60. The Devils will attempt to close with the team, bringing all guns to bear. Lacking mounted weaponry, they are limited to the weapons they carry. If they try to drive and fight during the same action, add a +2 Target Modifier to all action attempts. Combat will last for five Vehicle Turns, when the team will be out of Devils territory, or until the team increases its lead to 100 meters or more. At the end of every Vehicle Turn, make a Vehicle (4) Test for any random player character. If no successes are rolled, the team has wandered into Tight Terrain (Restricted Terrain at night). On the next Vehicle Turn, roll again. If the team still has no successes, the characters remain in Tight Terrain. At the end of any turn in which the random team member scores 1 or more successes, the terrain returns to Restricted.

If the Devils successfully incapacitate the Runabout or any other auto, they will stop to loot. If the gangers stop the Runabout, the team should also stop to protect their Mr. Johnson. At this point, normal combat occurs.

Once combat has been resolved, the team can continue on to the meeting described in the next section, **Junk Yard Dogs**. If any player characters are wounded, they have about 20 minutes to attempt minor healing. Any additional time would make Topal late for the meet, and he will not allow that to happen.

DEBUGGING

If it looks as though the players' team is about to get trashed in their first combat encounter, the gamemaster may show them some mercy. Another gang can ride to the rescue, inadvertently, of course. Lone Star could even save them, but that is unlikely, given Lone Star's attitude toward inhabitants of the Barrens. If the team is really missing their rolls, give them a break. This encounter is purely to remind them how tough and dangerous is life in the Barrens. It should not result in their going to an early grave.

It is important that Topal remain alive until the next chapter. He needs to get to the junk yard to get things really rolling.

ASPHALT DEVILS

QUICK KILL

Always moving, always talking, Quick Kill is hyperactive. A real wild man.

Attributes

Body: 4 (5)
Quickness: 4
Strength: 5
Charisma: 3
Intelligence: 3
Willpower: 5
Essence: 3.5
Reaction: 3 (5)

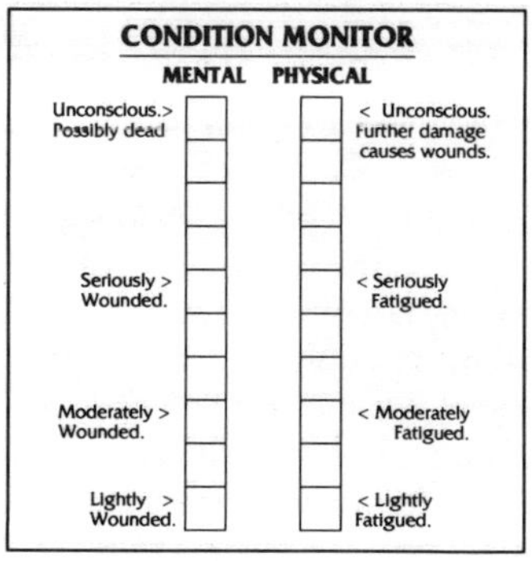

CONDITION MONITOR
MENTAL PHYSICAL
Unconscious.> Possibly dead
< Unconscious. Further damage causes wounds.
Seriously > Wounded.
< Seriously Fatigued.
Moderately > Wounded.
< Moderately Fatigued.
Lightly > Wounded.
< Lightly Fatigued.

Skills

Armed Combat: 4
Bike: 6
Firearms: 4
Gunnery: 3
Throwing Weapons: 3

Dice Pools

Defense (Armed): 4
Defense (Unarmed): 1
Dodge: 4

Cyberware

Cybereyes with Low-Light
Dermal Plating (1)
Wired Reflexes (1)

Gear

2 Offensive Grenades (6M3)
Ares Predator [10 (clip), 2 extra clips, Laser Sight, 4M2]
Harley Scorpion
Helmet (1/1)
Katana (+1 Reach, 5M3)
Lined Coat (4/2)
Uzi III SMG [16 (clip), 2 extra clips, Laser Sight, 4M3]

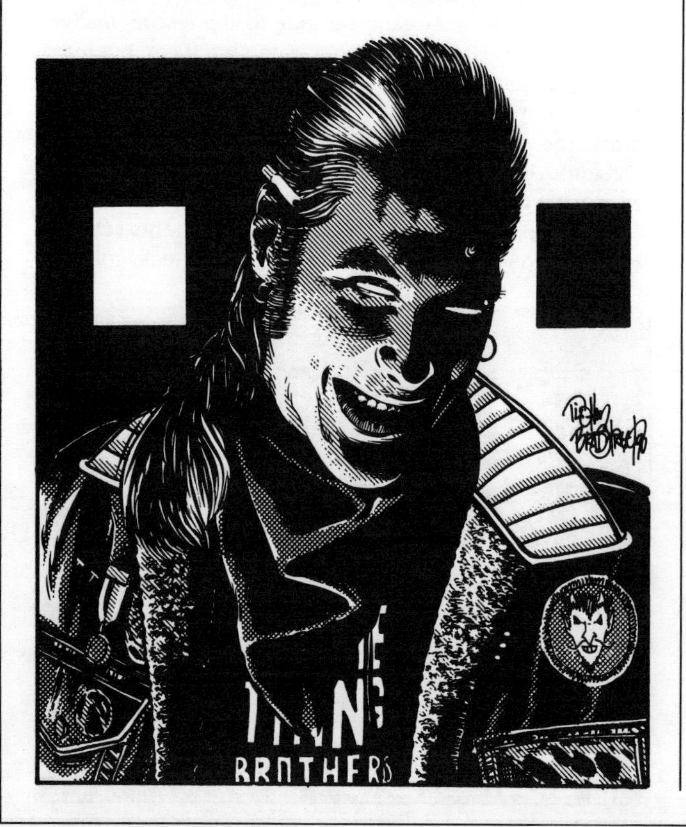

SWEET SHEILA

Quick Kill's honey, Sheila is anything but sweet in battle. She screams like a maniac during a fight, seeming, oddly enough, prettier that way.

Attributes

Body: 3
Quickness: 4
Strength: 4
Charisma: 5
Intelligence: 3
Willpower: 6
Essence: 6
Reaction: 3

CONDITION MONITOR
MENTAL PHYSICAL
Unconscious.> Possibly dead
< Unconscious. Further damage causes wounds.
Seriously > Wounded.
< Seriously Fatigued.
Moderately > Wounded.
< Moderately Fatigued.
Lightly > Wounded.
< Lightly Fatigued.

Skills

Bike: 7
Firearms: 4
Stealth: 5
Unarmed Combat: 2

Dice Pools

Defense (Armed): 1
Defense (Unarmed): 2
Dodge: 4

Gear

Armor Jacket (5/3)
Heckler & Koch HK227 SMG [20 (clip), 2 extra clips, Laser Sight, 5M3]
Harley Scorpion

OTHER GANG MEMBERS

CONDITION MONITOR
MENTAL PHYSICAL
Unconscious.> Possibly dead
< Unconscious. Further damage causes wounds.
Seriously > Wounded.
< Seriously Fatigued.
Moderately > Wounded.
< Moderately Fatigued.
Lightly > Wounded.
< Lightly Fatigued.

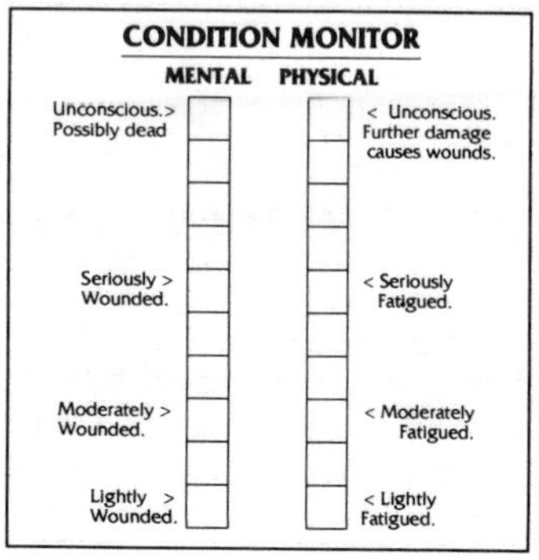

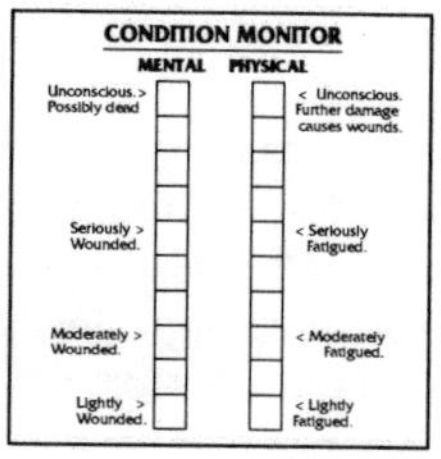

Attributes

Body: 4
Quickness: 4
Strength: 4
Charisma: 3
Intelligence: 2
Willpower: 3
Essence: 6
Reaction: 3

Skills

Armed Combat: 4
Bike: 4
Firearms: 3
Unarmed Combat: 4

Dice Pools

Defense (Armed): 4
Defense (Unarmed): 4
Dodge: 4

Gear

Armor Vest with Plating (4/3)
Knife (2L1)
Uzi III SMG [16 (clip), 2 extra clips, 4M3]
Yamaha Rapier

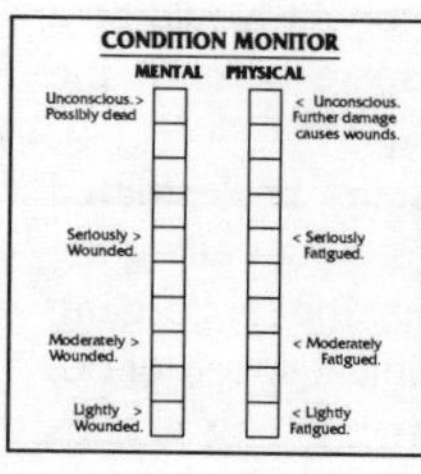

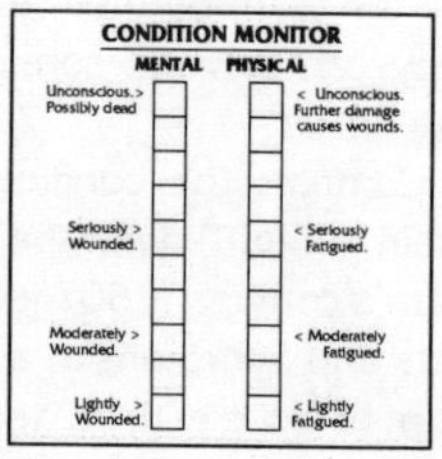

CONDITION MONITOR
MENTAL PHYSICAL
Unconscious.> Possibly dead
< Unconscious. Further damage causes wounds.
Seriously > Wounded.
< Seriously Fatigued.
Moderately > Wounded.
< Moderately Fatigued.
Lightly > Wounded.
< Lightly Fatigued.

CONDITION MONITOR
MENTAL PHYSICAL
Unconscious.> Possibly dead
< Unconscious. Further damage causes wounds.
Seriously > Wounded.
< Seriously Fatigued.
Moderately > Wounded.
< Moderately Fatigued.
Lightly > Wounded.
< Lightly Fatigued.

CONDITION MONITOR
MENTAL PHYSICAL
Unconscious.> Possibly dead
< Unconscious. Further damage causes wounds.
Seriously > Wounded.
< Seriously Fatigued.
Moderately > Wounded.
< Moderately Fatigued.
Lightly > Wounded.
< Lightly Fatigued.

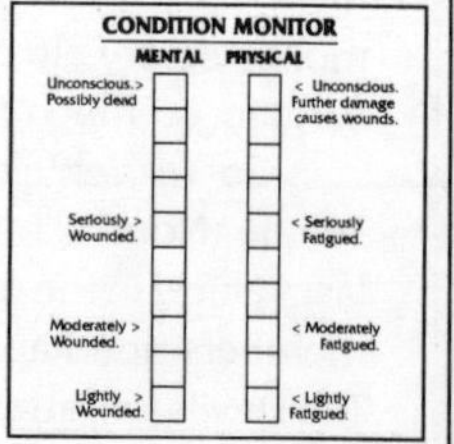

JUNK YARD DOGS

TELL IT TO THEM STRAIGHT

You follow Topal's lead to the gates of Black's Junk Yard, one of Seattle's legendary establishments. Beyond the heavy steel gate are mounds of cars and ancient vehicles whose fate has taken them to a final resting place in Black's. Topal stops the car. Illuminated by the lights of his Runabout, he heads for the fencing that runs along the massive junk yard. Apparently oblivious to the danger of standing in the light, he bends low over a single round rock next to the fence. With a heave of his shoulders, the portly man rolls the large rock away, revealing a tunnel under the fence. It will be a tight fit for Topal, but he literally dives in, case in hand. You turn off the lights on the Runabout, glancing around furtively. You can easily hide your own vehicles behind the dumpsters in the alley across the street. Within moments, you are dismounted and crowded around the tunnel entrance. Putting aside your massive doubts and suspicions, you slip into the dank, grimy opening.

Fortunately, the tunnel widens considerably after the entrance. After you slide along on your stomach for about five meters, the tunnel suddenly turns sharply upward. You crawl out into the moonlight just in time to see Topal setting the red hood of an ancient Ford LTD against a rusting stack of compressed cars. The mounds of junk leaning against the yard's fence effectively conceal the tunnel exit. Signaling wordlessly for you to follow, Topal heads off between the rows of cars.

You creep through the twisted maze of vehicle parts, forced to retrace your steps several times because of fallen stacks of cars blocking the way. Just when you're wondering if Topal really knows where he's going, he puts a finger to his lips and motions a stop deep within the labyrinthine junk yard.

"Good, good, good. We are here at last," he whispers. You stare out into a roughly circular clearing. Spare parts litter the beaten grass. The full moon casts shadows along the clearing's edge, making it impossible to tell whether the darker spots are truly openings within the perimeter or if they are a deeper recess.

If a team member astrally examines the meeting place:

You begin your trance, letting the ability that is yours alone gradually take control. You feel your body rising as you look about. At first glance, the meeting place appears empty. On second look, you see three persons, possibly Elves, across the clearing. The first is leaning against a shape you take for a car. What may be a rifle rests on one side of him, a slim leather briefcase rests on the other.

The second individual sits in lotus position atop the tallest stack of metal in the area. From his vantage point, he has an almost unlimited view of the clearing. He is surrounded by a faint blue aura, the obvious effect of some spell. Twin pulses of yellow light also run across his body, almost as though playing tag. These lights create the illusion of a secondary yellow aura. In his lap is a hunk of metal you take to be a gun.

The final figure's astral form floats above and slightly behind the standing Elf. She, too, is bathed in a faint blue aura. As your eyes lock, she nods at you. Your astral vision senses nobody and nothing else of interest.

When the team is ready for the meet:

Topal peers cautiously into the clearing. Breathing deeply, he is just about to step forward when a figure appears across the clearing. The other man's left hand is empty. In his right, he carries a slim leather briefcase. As he moves into the light, his dark Elven features are clearly visible. He plucks the cigarette hanging from the corner of his mouth and flings it toward the tunnel opening in a single, smooth gesture.

"Are you ready, Raven-man? I am here for the trade." The Elf's voice is clear, precise, carrying easily across the distance.

Topal looks around in obvious fear. "This is wrong. All

wrong. Take this." With a grace and swiftness belying his size, he removes the wrist cuff and quickly places it on the wrist of the nearest team member. "It will be safe with you. Enter the circle when I say. Not a moment sooner."

Topal enters the circle, but after a few steps, he begins to wheeze. A few more steps and he slows to barely a walk. He struggles his way to the Elf and stands shakily before him. "You are not the one with whom I made the deal. Where is the other?"

"You deal with me, Raven-man. I have the oath price. Where is your part of the bargain?"

BEHIND THE SCENES

Have the team members each make a Perception/Intelligence (6) Test. Roll also for Topal and the three Elven NPCs. Anyone with Cyberears/Hearing Amplification active gets a modifier of +1.

PERCEPTION TEST

Successes	Result
1 or less	A wall of cars comes cascading down as a Lone Star Citymaster pushes into the perimeter of the clearing. High-intensity headlights scatter the shadows as the rear door drops to the ground with a thump. The turret on top of the vehicle swivels in your direction. You turn to see several heavily armed street cops charging up the metal corridor in your direction. "Turn to ice, boys and girls. You're all under arrest." (Characters with 1 success or less are surprised.)
3 – 2	In the distance, you hear the throaty rumble of a heavy vehicle. It seems to be moving very quickly in your direction. (Characters with 3 – 2 Successes will not be surprised, but enter the Combat Turn through normal Initiative.)
4+	In the distance, you can hear the faint, but distinctive rumble of an approaching vehicle. There are other sounds, too, among the cars and in the air. Trouble is afoot. (Characters with 4+ successes are not surprised and may take one Action before Lone Star arrives.)

The NPCs will take the following actions as they are able. Bloodwing will jump out of the clearing, leaping into the shadows behind him. From there, he will get his HAR and snipe at Topal, believing that the Raven shaman has double-crossed him. Once Topal goes down, Bloodwing beats a hasty retreat.

Tundra will attempt to fry Topal with a Power Bolt. If the shaman is still standing, the Elf will lob both grenades into the clearing and take off with Bloodwing.

Harper will cover the retreat of her partners, sniping with the Enfield or else casting Chaotic World if the opportunity presents itself.

Topal stands confused at first, then makes a frantic attempt to get away, running wildly in any direction. Unless the team enters the clearing and pulls him to safety, he *will* be killed either by the Elves or by a stray shot from Lone Star.

Lone Star arrives in force, a Citymaster on the ground deploying ten troopers and supported by a pair of Yellowjackets that silently descend into the area via autorotation. As the Citymaster comes into view, the helicopters engage their engines and spotlights. A handful of Lone Star troopers is also scattered around the junk yard, but these should be used only as needed.

As his forces arrive, Captain Grissim's voice blares out over the Citymaster's loudspeaker: "All right, Bloodwing. We've got you and your terrorist compadres surrounded. Give it up now and we may only beat the drek out of you." Fortunately for the runners, Lone Star's first priority is Bloodwing.

Once the Elves kill Topal and begin their getaway, the runners are on their own in attempting to get away. Initially, one Lone Star street cop bars the way of each team member. Once the team member fights his way past the cop, he can and should attempt to flee. If combat lasts for four or more rounds, another cop will move in to assist in the capture. This means that a new cop enters combat at the start of every fifth turn. Impress upon the team that this is a major raid, designed to capture the participants of the predawn meeting. If the runners stay and fight, they will be overwhelmed by numbers alone.

When team members attempt to flee, have them make a Reaction (5) Test. Apply the following results.

REACTION TEST

Successes	Result
0	Cornered by a Lone Star cop, the team member must fight his way clear. If the fight is not concluded within 5 turns, another cop joins the fray. Once clear of all opponents, roll 1D6. On a 1 – 2 result, go to the 3– 4 successes result. On a 3 – 4, go to the 5 – 6 successes below; on a 5 – 6 result, go to 7+ successes below.
1 – 2	Evading the patrolling street cops, the runner joins up with another team member. Using the first die roll for both of them, they go to 0 successes.
3 – 4	The player character comes to the wall of the junk yard. To climb over, he makes an Athletics (5) Test. No successes indicates failure; 1 success means he has climbed the wall, but is subject to 4M2 damage from the razor wire. Two or more successes allows him to successfully scale the wall.
5 – 6	The player character comes to the front gate of the junk yard. He may attempt to climb over. He makes an Athletics (4) Test. With 1 or more successes, he successfully climbs over the gate.
7+	The runner arrives back at the entry tunnel and may crawl through and escape.

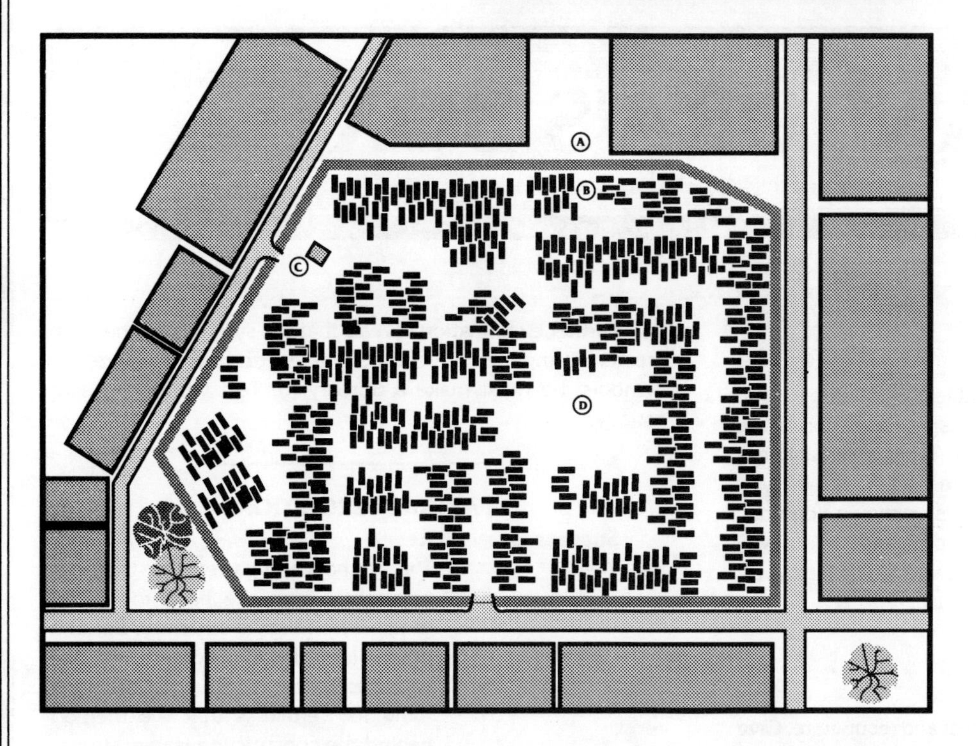

Black's Junk Yard

A = Tunnel Entrance
B = Tunnel Exit
C = Citymaster Entrance
D = Meeting Place
□ = 5 meters
= wrecked cars

Note that in the confusion, team members may not initially start their escape together. They can, however, link up during the course of the escape. Team members traveling together may roll only once to check their location, using the slowest Reaction among them as the target number.

It is unlikely the team members will encounter Bloodwing or his partners. If they do, the statistics for the Elves and for Grissim, leader of the Lone Star forces, are in the **Cast of Characters** chapter.

Once the team successfully manages to escape, they will probably want to hole up somewhere nearby. No matter where they finally decide to go, proceed to the next chapter, **Pandora's Box**.

DEBUGGING

Several things should happen during this encounter. The team, or most of it, should get away and Topal must die. It's tough, but Topal's time has come.

If some team members are captured, allow them a chance to get away as the cops are marching them toward the patrol cars parked at the front gate. If any team member still cannot escape, arrest him, book him for trespassing, and lock him up. He will be detained for 24 hours while Grissim interrogates him under the professional eye of a Lone Star mage with Analyze Truth. When the time is up, Grissim is confused, but convinced that the runner knows nothing about Bloodwing. He will order the character released but placed under round-the-clock astral surveillance.

Topal can expire in a number of interesting ways. The Elves will most likely kill him, but if not, a stack of cars can fall on him or he can simply disappear into the maze of rusted vehicles, where Bloodwing will do him in. As a last resort, Bloodwing can pick him off as Topal is about to get back into his car and make good his escape.

STREET COPS

These underpaid employees of Lone Star just want to get through the night alive. If they are seriously wounded, they will stay down and let somebody else make the collar. They have been told to apprehend Bloodwing but not to get killed doing it. As a result, they will always use their stun batons first. If things get really bad, they will pull out the heavier firepower. Note that these cops are a cut above the run-of-the-mill corp cops in Seattle, having been trained in riot duty and close combat.

Attributes
- Body: 4
- Quickness: 4
- Strength: 5
- Charisma: 2
- Intelligence: 3
- Willpower: 3
- Essence: 6
- Reaction: 3

Skills
- Armed Combat: 4
- Etiquette (Street): 3
- Firearms: 3
- Unarmed Combat: 4

Special Skill
- Police Procedure: 4

Dice Pools
- Defense (Armed): 4
- Defense (Unarmed): 4
- Dodge: 4

Gear
- Ares Predator [10 (clip), 2 extra clips, 4M2]
- Armor Jacket (5/3)
- Earplug Radio
- Helmet (1/1)
- Low-Light Goggles
  - Stun Baton (+1 Reach, 5L2 Stun + Special)

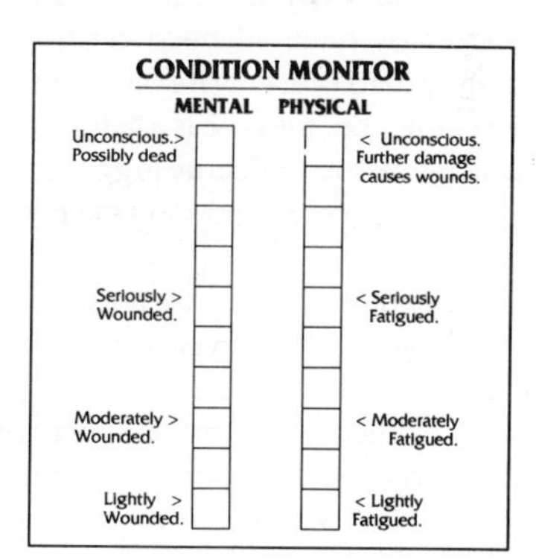

TELL IT TO THEM STRAIGHT

You arrive at your destination breathless, but pumped with adrenaline. To calm your nerves, you focus your attention on the many problems at hand. The former Mr. Topal is certainly not going to be paying you the rest of your fee, but he has left you with a parting gift: the alloy case and its unknown contents. Time to take care of business. You should probably find out why Lone Star was there at Black's, who else was at the junk yard, and check out the suddenly ownerless case.

BEHIND THE SCENES

The team should take this time to rest and recuperate. Give them most of the day, until 6:00 P.M., to prepare for the remainder of the adventure. If need be, they can go to any of the local clinics. They can also check out word on the street or examine the case. Any additional events can be handled as needed, but at 6:00 P.M. things start to roll.

If the player characters want to do some checking into the why and who of things, go to the **Legwork** section.

EXAMINING THE BRIEFCASE

The case itself is quite harmless and can be opened easily. It was designed to keep its contents safe, but the exterior safeguards have all been destroyed by now, either by the journey to its present site or in some other way. If the characters are interested, the case is a fairly common courier design readily available at most security luggage shops. Examination from the Astral Plane reveals nothing except a slight glow of power from within.

Opening the case by twisting the locks and lifting the top will reveal a large, carved wooden box just slightly smaller than the inner dimensions of the case. If a character succeeds at a Magical Theory (6) Test, he recognizes some of the symbols etched on the case as derivative of ancient Kabbalistic symbols. Though similar, these symbols cannot be directly translated. The box itself is in good shape, showing little wear and tear.

The cover of the box is notched to the bottom and can be lifted off easily. Inside is a piece of black silk draped over the contents of the box. Removing the slightly musty silk reveals the idol. It was Topal who placed this piece of silk in the box.

As previously described, the idol is nestled in the center fold of a black cloth pillow, which is embroidered with many odd symbols and patterns that *are not* related to the symbols on the box. Examination via Astral Perception will reveal the presence of magic in the cloth and an impenetrable black sphere, much like that made by a hermetic circle, surrounding the idol.

Further examination reveals that the symbols on the cloth are generating the sphere. If a character attempts to analyze the symbols, he must make a Sorcery (6) Test while assensing astrally.

ASTRAL PERCEPTION

Successes	Result
1 – 2	The symbols and patterns on the cloth apparently form the basis for a hermetic-style magical structure, but at a power level far exceeding what one would expect for an area that size. One thing for certain is that the method behind the construction is very strong, indeed.
3 – 4	The magical structure appears to be a barrier of some sort, but its nature is only similar to that generated by a hermetic circle.
5 – 6	Though complex and beyond the ken of the viewing character to understand, it is apparent that the magic's structure is unraveling.
7+	Strangely, the power of the spell seems to be turned *inward,* working to keep something inside, rather than protecting it from external forces.

In order to examine the idol properly, the players must remove it from the box. Doing so will produce no immediate, overt reaction.

The idol is carved from deep-red stone and is cool to the touch. It is vaguely demonic-looking, with glowing eyes and clutching to its body a pinkish globe. The odd patterns and symbols that cover it have no resemblance to those on either the wooden case or the pillow on which it rested. The idol is worn nearly smooth, perhaps from handling, perhaps from the elements, leaving the patterns and symbols barely visible.

For further examination of the idol, see the section, **Playing With Darkness**.

At 6:00 P.M., one of the runners receives a hurried phone call. He recognizes the voice as one of his contacts, but the fellow has never sounded so serious.

"Hey, chummer. You've got to move, and I mean now! Mr. Blue is about to pay you a special visit. Get out, but don't come here. You've attracted some heavy flies and I don't need that kind of trouble. Got it? I'll see you in a couple of days, if you live that long."

In the street outside, the runners see the hurried, but silent approach of several Lone Star patrol cars. From the looks of the gear the cops are carrying, the kid gloves have just come off. The gamemaster should allow the player characters to escape, but only by a hair.

From here, the team proceeds to the next section, **Turned Out, Tuned In**.

DEBUGGING

Only a few areas bear special attention at this point. If the characters choose not to handle the idol or use it, either now or later in the adventure, that's fine. The adventure can continue intact even if none of them falls under the object's influence, but it will certainly be more interesting if they do. The gamemaster should make the power of the idol as tempting as possible, maybe even force the runners into a situation later where one of the characters is all but forced to use it to save their collective butt.

If the team plans to separate during the day, have them choose a meeting place for later. If still in separate locations by 6:00 P.M., they will get the word via separate channels. The team should realize there is safety in numbers. If not, try to get them together as soon as possible.

See the **Playing With Darkness** section for ideas on how to build tension once one of the runners has handled the idol.

TELL IT TO THEM STRAIGHT

You decide to take to the streets, where smart types like you can get lost in the crowd. You are trying to decide what to do next when something in the vid store across the street catches your eye. If you didn't know better, you'd swear that was your face on the nightly news.

You cross the street to check out the report. As you watch, an old picture of you dissolves into fuzzy images of the other members of the team. A voice cautions the populace that you present a grave menace to them.

"Be advised. These individuals are armed and should be considered extremely dangerous. They have already clashed with Lone Star forces, leaving several officers injured. Consider these individuals to be Class A felons. If you spot any or all of them, do not attempt..."

So much for hiding on the streets, chummer. The crowd suddenly doesn't seem so cozy. In fact, you're feeling mighty conspicuous. You duck into an alley to assess the situation. Seems like you need an alternate plan.

BEHIND THE SCENES

The team is being pursued by a very confused Captain Grissim, among others. Grissim's superiors have ordered him to use any means necessary to bring the runners in, alive, if possible. Grissim insisted that the runners were small fish who had nothing to do with Bloodwing, but to no avail. Despite misgivings, he alerted the media as soon as he was able to identify Topal and to trace his activities of the last few days. Grissim's boss expects results and the Captain does not disappoint him.

From here, the team has several options, none of them appealing. If any player characters try to return to their homes, a Lone Star welcoming committee will be waiting to greet them. Cops at these places will play it safe, calling for backup first and attempting to apprehend second. Play any such encounters using the **Lone Star Country** section, p. 22.

If the runners go to any of their usual spots, they will probably be stopped at the door. Nobody wants the kind of trouble they're bringing these days. Should the player characters manage to get inside, one and all will avoid them. If the team continues to wander the streets, some squatter will recognize them and use his last nuyen to snitch to Lone Star, who will respond in a matter of minutes.

If the team keeps moving, they should be all right, but remaining on the street, even in a car, will eventually attract more and more Lone Star activity. If the team attempts to get to an abandoned building or to sneak into a location where they are not known, they will be safe. Unless they keep their heads down and out of sight, they will eventually be captured.

If the runners attempt to find out what's going on, see the **Legwork** section.

Part of the reason the team is getting the cold shoulder has to do with Bloodwing, who has spread rumors that the team killed Topal to keep the idol for themselves. A person can get away with many things while shadowrunning in 2050, but icing an employer is not one of them. Such a deed places a runner somewhere below a diseased squatter on the food chain. Unfortunately for the team, Topal's oldest friend, Caw Caw, believes the rumors and has gathered together the Children of Sophocles to find the runners and avenge their dead friend.

At this point, the players need to clear their names, but they should also be curious enough to find out more about the strange object suddenly in their care. If they take the talisman to a professional shaman, talismonger, or mage, they may be able to get some help. See **The Idol**, in **Legwork**, p.41.

Depending on what the players do or do not do here (or on what the gamemaster decides), the adventure can proceed either to **Old Dog, New Trix**, **Lone Star Country**, or even **Children In The Streets**. Even if some of the runners' contacts have fingered them several times (see **Legwork**), the team only has to go up against Lone Star once. Of course, they may encounter the cops again because of actions in other sections.

DEBUGGING

This situation should be hard on the team. If someone is not showing them hostility, that person is likely to turn them over to the cops. This should force the runners to rely on themselves, not lead to open confrontation. If they are smart, they will avoid the cops and stay clear of people who don't want them around. If they don't see the wisdom in that, rough them up a bit. Make their lives miserable. Impound their cars and bikes, seal their homes, and send a few goons after them. They will get the hint eventually. If the team is especially dense, you can run **Lone Star Country** as many times as needed. The adventure should not turn into a slugfest with the cops, however.

OLD DOG, NEW TRIX

TELL IT TO THEM STRAIGHT

You gaze at the simple shop across the street. Its threadbare awning stretches out over the sidewalk like a shroud. The opaque windows reveal nothing except the crude astrological symbols painted on them. Could this really be the place?

If a team member examines the shop astrally:

From outside, the store is inert. Mundane.

You glide across the street, through a passing bus, and enter the store. You can see immediately that it has been converted from a shop to a home. There is a simple sitting area, filled with furniture, books, and dozens of small forms that you take to be dogs. Sitting near the fireplace, a woman sits, rocking slowly in place. You think she is knitting. A few trinkets of little power hang from her body.

You are about to leave when you notice that all the dogs are staring at you.

When the team enters the shop:

Keeping an eye open for trouble, you move across the street to the front of the small shop. A carved wooden sign announces: "Trixy, Knower of Secrets, Teller of Fates. Fortunes told 10:30 – 6:00. Closed Sundays and Holidays." Well, at least Trixy's practical, whoever she is.

Just then, an ancient hand reaches under the shade and flips the sign in the window. Trixy's is now open for business. One final look around and you open the door into a small, dark vestibule. As the door closes behind you, the latch falling into place, a small woman appears in the opposite doorway. You can barely see her face in the dark, but you can tell she is very old. She gazes calmly at your motley crew.

"Ah, early customers. Business should be brisk today." She smiles up at the nearest runner, pausing slightly. "You had better come in and tell me all about it, youngster. I can see in your eyes that you're in very deep doo-doo."

BEHIND THE SCENES

Trixy is one of the oldest shamans in Seattle, having been a fortune teller for most of her life. She has, however, stayed away from the more traditional forms of divination, relying more on her own common sense and interpretation of the signs of nature around her.

When the team enters the shop, Trixy is not surprised. Though she did not know exactly who to expect, her dreams have told her to prepare for the coming of the team. While the runners make themselves comfortable, Trixy retires to the kitchen, returning moments later with a tray of pastries and a kettle of tea.

Refreshments served, Trixy settles into an overstuffed chair to hear the team's story. She says little, preferring to listen to the full story first. When the runners are done, she asks several questions, then sits back to think for a moment. When she asks to see the case, any runner (or runners) affected by the idol will become slightly nervous for no apparent reason. If he is hostile, Trixy will back down and attempt another approach. If the runner does not press his hostility toward her or if he is under better control, she will ask to see the idol. Assuming someone hands it to her, she holds it for only a short time, during which the three dozen or so dogs become visibly restless. Without a word, she hands the idol back to the runners.

At this point, Trixy nods several times, then asks the runners to come back a couple of hours after she has had time to think. If they wish to remain here, she will agree. Regardless of whether they go or stay, she will put on her coat and hat and go for a walk, accompanied by the two largest dogs.

Should the runners search Trixy's home in her absence, they will learn enough to guess that she is a Dog shaman. They will find nothing else of interest. While waiting for Trixy's return, they can pass a quiet few hours. Food and drinks are available in the kitchen and abundant reading material is scattered throughout the house. If the team decides to leave, this would be a perfect time for **Children In The Streets** or **Lone Star Country**. If the gamemaster prefers, he can allow them simply to leave now and return for their meeting.

When Trixy returns, she has with her an extra dog, who joins the pack in the living room as if he had always belonged. If the runners are present, she will begin. If not, she will await their return.

When they are all present, Trixy's face takes on a strange, somber look. She settles in her chair, straightening her back and neck. In a deep, resonant voice, she begins to speak. "I have meditated on your problems and see that you are right to be concerned both for your own safety and the safety of those around you. The object you carry is dangerous. I am not sure of exactly what it is, but I see signs of malevolent intelligence and all-consuming darkness. It is a tool of corruption. All who come in contact with it are threatened.

"As far as I can tell, there are several ways to destroy the idol, but only one true, certain way: you must take it to a Dragon. There are others who know the ways of its destruction, but they might be tempted by its power, and may, in fact, already be. Only a Dragon is wise enough and understands enough to simply destroy it.

"You must find a Dragon and deliver the idol to him, but be careful. This is not a deal, but a request of a service from the Dragon. Do not think you can trade the idol, because this is not the case. I am truly sorry you have come to possess such a terrible artifact, but it is your fate. Deliver it to a Dragon and you may yet come out of this whole and safe."

The runners will probably feel like somebody up there doesn't like them, which could well be the case. By now, they should have figured out that possessing the idol is a no-win situation. The only good thing is that now they have a clear direction in which to travel.

If someone thinks to ask, Trixy can suggest a Dragon to contact. His name is Geyswain and he runs Lochlann Investments, an investment and real estate corporation located along the Tacoma waterfront. Though Geyswain is young, he can probably help the team out. Because Trixy knows him, she can probably get the team in to see him later that day. She knows of only one other Dragon in the Seattle area: Haesslich, security chief for United Oil. Trixy has heard that he is out of town, however. It will not take much checking—no die rolls required—to learn that Haesslich is, in fact, in Tokyo on business.

To avoid complications, the gamemaster will find it best if no other Dragons in the Seattle area are available or interested. If the team contacts Geyswain independently, he will agree to see them later that same day. Though the player characters may never know it, Trixy has already contacted Geyswain.

Trixy would like to help more, but her advanced age makes it difficult to successfully run the shadows. If the team asks, she will decline an offer to accompany them. Nor she will agree to take the idol under any circumstance short of the team's death.

From here, if the runners have not yet run into the Children of Sophocles, the group is primed and ready for action in **Children In The Streets**. If the team has already met with the Children but have not run afoul of the law, they can proceed directly to **Penthouse Suite** for a meet with the Dragon Geyswain. If the cops are on their tail, go to **Lone Star Country**. Of course, the team can always try to learn more by talking with Contacts, but that is still a risky proposition. See **Legwork.**

DEBUGGING

The team may fail to see that taking the idol to a Dragon, namely Geyswain, should be their next move. Events will not progress very much until the team takes that step. Meanwhile, Blackwing, Grissim, and a mysterious lady are all on the team's tail, each getting closer to the final confrontation.

About the only other thing they can mess up at this point is that they might get on Trixy's bad side. It would be hard to do, as she is a patient lady, but it is possible. If they are heading down the wrong road, remind them that Trixy is the only person who can help them clear their reputations. No rep, no work. If they are still uppity, let them walk. All roads lead to this shaman. If the team attacks her for some unknown reason, they may be able to take her, but their days are numbered. Try to head off the situation before it comes to pass.

TRIXY

Trixy, which is the only name she goes by, grew up in what is now the Redmond Barrens of Seattle. She has lived in the same building for 60 years, becoming almost a neighborhood fixture. Trixy is an ex-fortune teller. She still maintains a small shop in the front of her apartment, but more out of habit than the prospect of a client. Trixy is a well-loved, well-respected member of her community, though few suspect the power she wields. She would never complain about the hard life she has led, but it has reduced her Essence and Magic Attributes to 4.

Attributes
- Body: 2
- Quickness: 1
- Strength: 1
- Charisma: 5
- Intelligence: 6
- Willpower: 5
- Essence: 4
- Magic: 4
- Reaction: 3

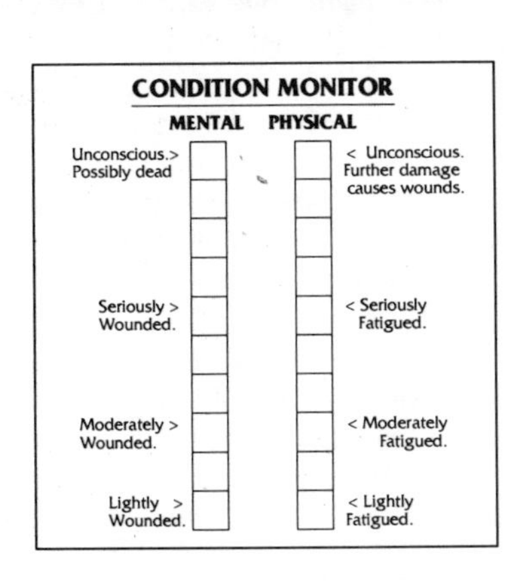

Skills
- Armed Combat: 3
- Biotech: 2
- Conjuring: 7
- Etiquette (Street): 6
- Magical Theory: 6
- Psychology: 2
- Sorcery: 6

Dice Pools
- Astral: 16
- Defense (Armed): 3
- Defense (Unarmed): 1
- Dodge: 1
- Magic: 6

Gear
- Dodge Scoot
- Lined Coat (4/2)
- Medicine Lodge Materials (8)
- Ordinary Clothing
- Orichalcum Knife (3)
- Reusable Fetishes for all Spells
- Ritual Sorcery Materials: Detection (6)
- Ritual Sorcery Materials: Health (6)
- Trauma Patches (2)

Totem
- Dog

Spells

Combat:
- Mana Ball: 6
- Power Dart: 5
- Sleep: 8

Detection
- Analyze Truth: 6
- Clairvoyance: 8
- Detect Enemies: 6
- Mind Probe: 8

Health
- Antidote Severe Toxin: 4
- Heal Moderate Wounds: 5
- Heal Severe Wounds: 4

Manipulation
- Hibernate: 5
- Levitate Person: 5

TELL IT TO THEM STRAIGHT

You are walking down the street, head low, eyes on your shoes. You don't want any more trouble than you've already got. Squatters and wage slaves dodge aside as you clear a path among the rabble of society.

Suddenly you hear the screeching of tires and the slamming of heavy car doors. You know what that means before even bothering to turn around. Lone Star has caught up with you. Turning swiftly, you see several armed street cops in all their glory. A single leader, probably an officer, hangs slightly back, shouting and pointing at you. The cops draw their clubs and begin to advance. Squatters clear a circle around you. It looks as though you have just become the evening's entertainment.

BEHIND THE SCENES

This chapter is for all the times the runners meet the long arm of the law. That could occur at any point during the adventure when the gamemaster decides the player characters have not kept out of sight enough or have been dumb enough to commit some other blunder that would attract the attention of Lone Star.

The actual encounter will occur wherever appropriate, whether as a result of a player-character error or through random chance. In cases where Lone Star arrived because of a tip, or in circumstances where they have ample time to call in reinforcements, the troopers show up in either multiple patrol cars or a single Citymaster. There are two street cops per runner present, and a single Lieutenant for every four or so troopers.

The cops always advance cautiously in the beginning, attempting to judge the runners' intent. If present, the Lieutenant will do all the talking. If the team puts up a fight, the cops respond with equal force. If the runners pull guns, the cops first dive for cover and then pull their own weapons. The runners should realize that Lone Star has enough assets to field what is effectively a small military unit, should they perceive the threat to be significant enough. If the runners keep the combat simple, the cops will use only their clubs.

If, however, any Lone Star trooper was seriously injured or killed in the Black's Junk Yard fight, Lone Star will take off the kid gloves and assume that the runners are always armed, dangerous, and homicidal.

If the team tries to run, one cop driver per car and the Lieutenant will return to the vehicles and give chase. The remainder of the cops will chase on foot. The team can surrender to Lone Star if they want. If they do, the squatters observing the fray will ridicule them, and the word will soon get around that the big, tough runners folded when push came to shove.

If the team is ever captured, they will be locked up and sent downtown. The police will confiscate all their armor, weapons, gadgets, the idol, and so on, leaving them to cool their jets in the lock-up. What happens next is up to the gamemaster. If the team has been doing well, give them a break. Otherwise, the gamemaster can squash them like bugs. A heavy fine and the loss of some, or all, of their gear should be pretty standard. Of course, if the player characters killed somebody, that is a another story.

Grissim wants to learn the truth about their connections to Bloodwing and so will interrogate the runners, as indicated in **Junk Yard Dogs**, p.13. If convinced of their relative innocence, the Captain might be willing to cut a deal with them to get Bloodwing. Of course, there is still the problem of the idol...

DEBUGGING

Though this is a combat encounter, do not let the team get out of hand. Flying bullets and grenades will quickly take out more bystanders than officers, bringing down more heat than the team can hope to fend off. Make sure the players know they are trying to get away. If quick enough, they may be able to give the cops the slip.

Lone Star Country should only be used to keep the heat on the runners. Make them sweat, make them worry, but don't make them dead.

LONE STAR LIEUTENANT

The Lieutenant is a veteran of the streets. He is usually called in when the action gets a little rougher. He provides the backup and brains to assist in the collar of dangerous felons.

The Lieutenant wants to keep the innocents safe and to put the baddies behind bars. He is firm and decisive and will always take that kind of action as the situation develops. If he errs, it is on the side of caution or safety.

Attributes
- Body: 5
- Quickness: 5
- Strength: 4
- Charisma: 4
- Intelligence: 5
- Willpower: 4
- Essence: 4.95
- Reaction: 5

Skills
- Armed Combat: 5
- Car: 4
- Etiquette (Street): 4
- Firearms: 5
- Negotiation: 3
- Unarmed Combat: 4

Special Skill
- Police Procedure: 5

Dice Pools
- Defense (Armed): 5
- Defense (Unarmed): 4
- Dodge: 5

Cyberware
- Cybereyes with Low-Light and Camera
- Radio

Gear
- Ares Predator [10 (clip), 2 extra clips, Laser Sight, 4M2]
- Armor Vest with Plating (4/3)
- Medkit
- Micro-recorder
- Plastic Restraints
- Stun Baton (+1 Reach, 5L2 Stun + Special)
- Trauma Patch (4)

LONE STAR STREET COPS

For a more complete description of the Lone Star Street Cop, see **Junk Yard Dogs**, page 15.

B	Q	S	C	I	W	E	M	R	Armor
4	4	5	2	3	3	6	—	3	6/4

Dice Pools: Defense (Armed) 4, Defense (Unarmed) 3, Dodge 4

Skills: Armed Combat 4, Etiquette (Street) 3, Firearms 3, Unarmed Combat 3

Special Skill: Police Procedure 4

Gear: Ares Predator [10 (clip), 2 extra clips, 4M2], Armor Jacket (5/3), Earplug Radio Helmet (1/1), Low-Light Goggles, Stun Baton (+1 Reach, 5L2 Stun +Special),

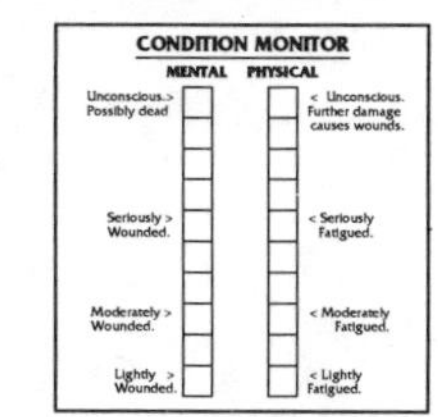
CONDITION MONITOR
MENTAL PHYSICAL
Unconscious.> Possibly dead
< Unconscious. Further damage causes wounds.
Seriously > Wounded.
< Seriously Fatigued.
Moderately > Wounded.
< Moderately Fatigued.
Lightly > Wounded.
< Lightly Fatigued.

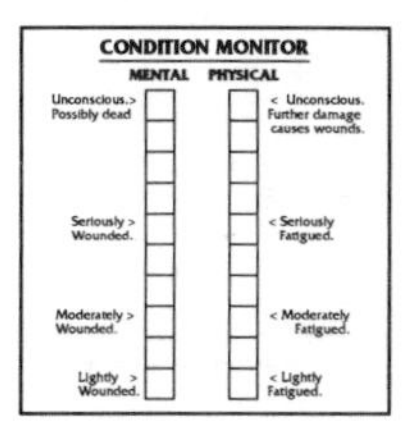
CONDITION MONITOR
MENTAL PHYSICAL
Unconscious.> Possibly dead
< Unconscious. Further damage causes wounds.
Seriously > Wounded.
< Seriously Fatigued.
Moderately > Wounded.
< Moderately Fatigued.
Lightly > Wounded.
< Lightly Fatigued.

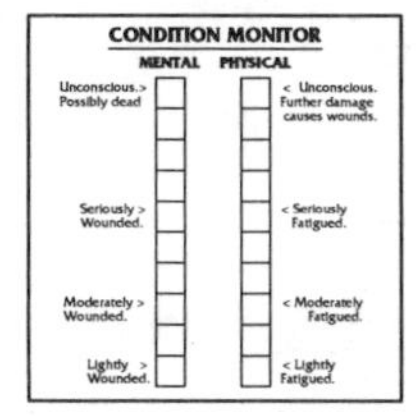
CONDITION MONITOR
MENTAL PHYSICAL
Unconscious.> Possibly dead
< Unconscious. Further damage causes wounds.
Seriously > Wounded.
< Seriously Fatigued.
Moderately > Wounded.
< Moderately Fatigued.
Lightly > Wounded.
< Lightly Fatigued.

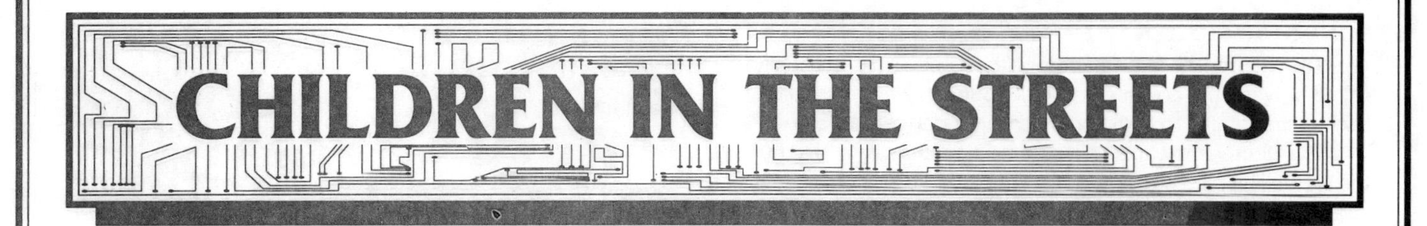

CHILDREN IN THE STREETS

TELL IT TO THEM STRAIGHT

The night air is chill, but no colder than the stares your so-called friends have been giving you. Fortunately, you seem to have given the cops the shake for the time being. The sidewalk is nearly empty, so it's easy to get by with little hassle. It's also easy for you to spot someone out of place.

BEHIND THE SCENES

Have each runner make an Unopposed Etiquette (Street) (4) Test to notice the Children of Sophocles making their move.

CHILDREN OF SOPHOCLES

Successes	Result
0	You notice a man walking toward you. He seems to be observing your group, but will not look anyone in the eye. You can see his left hand, but his right is concealed beneath his poncho. As you get closer, he slows his pace. (The character is surprised.)
1 – 2	You hear the clatter of running feet from behind you. Turning to look, you see a woman step behind a parked Jackrabbit, partially disappearing from sight. (The character is surprised.)
3 – 4	A man in front of you stops short, about five meters away. He stands still, one hand hidden under his poncho, as though waiting for something to happen. (The character is not surprised.)
5+	Across the street, you see a man who has been leaning casually against a wall until now. He looks around, then begins moving his hands in preparation for casting what you assume to be a spell. (The character is not surprised and may behave normally.)

The team has discovered the Children of Sophocles, or rather, the Children have discovered the team. Friends of Topal, these armchair mages and shaman are out to take revenge on the runners for the murder of their leader and possibly for the death of Simon Templeman. Under the leadership of Caw Caw, a Raven shaman, this group has been collecting information on the team. Believing the rumors spread by Bloodwing, the Children have finally tracked down the team.

The Children's plan is simple. They will trap the team against the row of buildings on the far side of the street and launch spells at the pinned runners. To keep the team from escaping, two of the Children will cover the left and right ends of the sidewalk, respectively. The remaining two will attack with their most powerful weapons or spells.

As they attack, Caw Caw and the Children curse the runners loudly for the deaths of Topal and Templeman. This should clue the runners to the fact that the Children are not really their enemies, but are simply misinformed. In fact, if the runners can forestall combat, they may learn valuable information and perhaps even obtain future aid from the Children of Sophocles.

Unfortunately for the Children, they are not really fighters. Though filled with righteous anger over the death of their friends, they do not have the combat skills to back up their attack. If the team puts up any resistance, the Children will have to back down. If one Children of Sophocles member is killed or two members are incapacitated, the fight is over. The others will surrender, throwing their weapons to the ground.

Assuming the runners win the fight, they can talk to the Children members to their heart's content. These pseudo-scholars are truly out of touch with the real world. Depending on how things go, this could be an opportunity to connect the runners with Trixy (see **Old Dog, New Trix,** p. 19). The Children know nothing of the idol because Topal, in his lust for power, did not tell his friends of his wondrous discovery. All Topal told them was that Simon Templeman was dead. And now Topal is, too. Knowing nothing of the idol, they will be as intrigued by it as were Topal and Templeman.

This may be the first time the runners hear of Simon Templeman. The Children can tell them that Templeman was a fellow scholar, a researcher recently returned from a prolonged archaeological/anthropological expedition through the South Pacific. They did not know he was back, however, until Topal informed them that their friend Simon was dead. They believe his death was due to natural causes, though it is perplexing because he had been in perfect health before his South Pacific trip.

To connect the runners to Trixy, have one of the Children say that he knows Trixy and that she has recently been asking around about a small object carved from red stone. That is all the Children member knows, but he can direct the runners to Trixy's if they ask.

DEBUGGING

The outcome of this encounter is solely in the runners' hands. If they're running so paranoid that they cannot stop to analyze why and wherefore events are transpiring this way, then so be it. Odds are the runners will be able to handle the Children of Sophocles team with little or no difficulty, but that is not the point. If they are paying attention, they should not have to deal with them in any other manner beyond conversation.

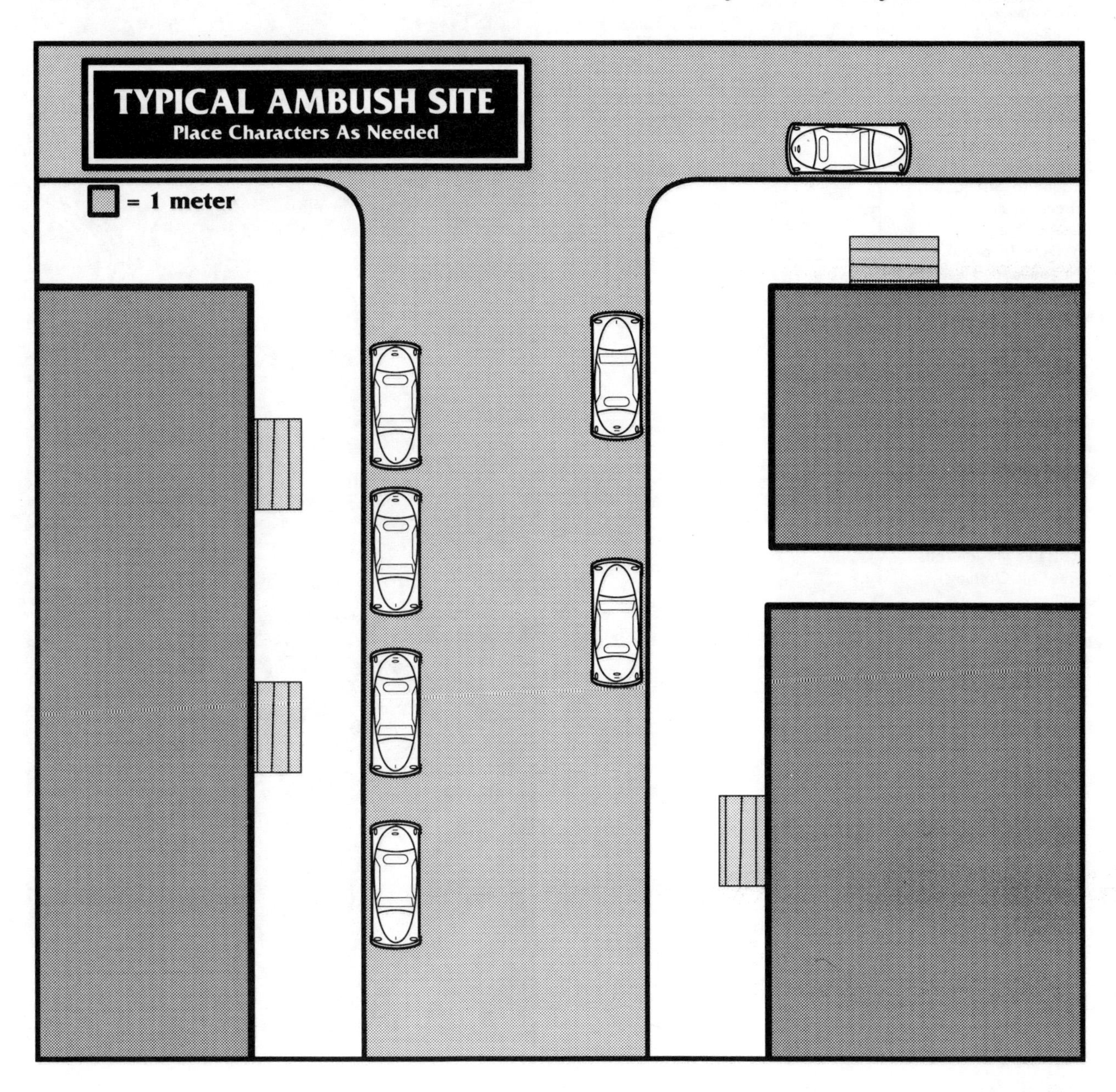

CHILDREN OF SOPHOCLES

CAW CAW

Caw Caw is cadaverously thin. All bones and skin, he leads the other members of the Children of Sophocles with eloquent, impassioned speeches. He was closest to Topal, and so it will be the hardest to persuade him of the team's innocence. Arrogant but not stupid, he believes that attacking the runners was the right thing to do.

Like all other Raven shaman, Caw Caw eats constantly, but food prepared only by the finest chefs in the city. His speaking voice is remarkable. Every word is uttered for maximum effect. He can easily sway crowds with his commanding voice.

Attributes
- Body: 3
- Quickness: 3
- Strength: 2
- Charisma: 2
- Intelligence: 4
- Willpower: 2
- Essence: 6
- Magic: 6
- Reaction: 3

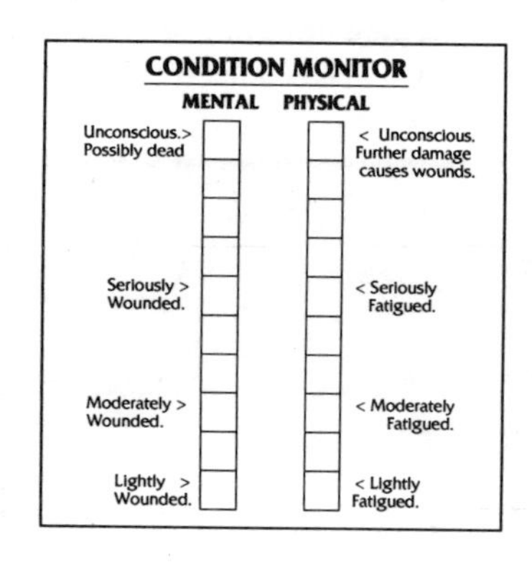
CONDITION MONITOR
MENTAL PHYSICAL
Unconscious.> Possibly dead | < Unconscious. Further damage causes wounds.
Seriously > Wounded. | < Seriously Fatigued.
Moderately > Wounded. | < Moderately Fatigued.
Lightly > Wounded. | < Lightly Fatigued.

Skills
- Conjuring: 4
- Etiquette (Street): 3
- Firearms: 2
- Leadership: 2
- Magical Theory: 6
- Negotiation: 3
- Sorcery: 3

Dice Pools
- Astral: 13
- Defense (Armed): 1
- Defense (Unarmed): 1
- Dodge: 3
- Magic: 3

Gear
- Armor Vest (2/1)
- Browning Max-Power [8 (clip), 1 spare clip, 4M2]
- Chrysler-Nissan Jackrabbit
- Reusable Detection Fetish
- Reusable Illusion Fetish
- Tres Chic Clothing

Totem
- Raven

Spells
- **Combat:**
  - Powerball: 5
- **Detection:**
  - Analyze Device: 4
- **Illusion:**
  - Chaotic World: 4
  - Entertainment: 3
- **Manipulation:**
  - Control Emotion: 3

GUNDERSON GREY KNIFE

Half Amerindian, Grey Knife is a hermetic mage who is interested in cause and effect. Analytical almost to a fault, he has an extreme dislike for coincidence. He diligently searches for the causes behind magic.

Attributes
- Body: 3
- Quickness: 4
- Strength: 3
- Charisma: 2
- Intelligence: 4
- Willpower: 4
- Essence: 6
- Magic: 6
- Reaction: 4

Skills
- Armed Combat: 4
- Conjuring: 4
- Etiquette (Street): 4
- Firearms: 3
- Magical Theory: 6
- Sorcery: 7

Dice Pools
- Astral: 17
- Defense (Armed): 4
- Defense (Unarmed): 1
- Dodge: 4
- Magic: 6

Gear
- Armor Poncho (as Lined Coat, 4/2)
- Enfield AS7 Shotgun [10 (clip), 4M3]
- Expendable Combat Fetishes (2)
- Knife (1L1)

Spells
- **Combat:**
  - Mana Bolt: 4
- **Manipulation:**
  - Armor: 6
  - Magic Fingers: 4

CONDITION MONITOR

	MENTAL	PHYSICAL	
Unconscious. > Possibly dead	☐	☐	< Unconscious. Further damage causes wounds.
	☐	☐	
	☐	☐	
	☐	☐	
Seriously > Wounded.	☐	☐	< Seriously Fatigued.
	☐	☐	
	☐	☐	
Moderately > Wounded.	☐	☐	< Moderately Fatigued.
	☐	☐	
Lightly > Wounded.	☐	☐	< Lightly Fatigued.

ORION YOSSARIAN

When it comes to street fighting, Yossarian is probably the most experienced of the Children, having done a stint as a magical bodyguard for an underworld crime figure some years ago. He is still not in a class anywhere near that of the runners, however.

Attributes
- Body: 3
- Quickness: 3
- Strength: 3
- Charisma: 4
- Intelligence: 5
- Willpower: 4
- Essence: 6
- Magic: 6
- Reaction: 4

Skills
- Car: 4
- Conjuring: 6
- Etiquette (Street): 4
- Firearms: 4
- Magical Theory: 4
- Sorcery: 6

Dice Pools
- Astral: 17
- Defense (Armed): 1
- Defense (Unarmed): 1
- Dodge: 3
- Magic: 6

Gear
- Ares Slivergun [30 (clip), Laser Sight, 2M3]
- Armor Jacket (5/3)
- Power Focus (3)

Spells

Combat:
- Power Bolt: 4

Detection:
- Detect Enemies: 4

Illusion:
- Mask: 3

Manipulation:
- Hibernate: 3
- Levitate Item: 4

CONDITION MONITOR

MENTAL		PHYSICAL	
Unconscious.> Possibly dead	☐	☐	< Unconscious. Further damage causes wounds.
	☐	☐	
	☐	☐	
	☐	☐	
Seriously > Wounded.	☐	☐	< Seriously Fatigued.
	☐	☐	
	☐	☐	
Moderately > Wounded.	☐	☐	< Moderately Fatigued.
	☐	☐	
Lightly > Wounded.	☐	☐	< Lightly Fatigued.

AEWYN CALEH

A female Elf, Caleh was known as Adrian until puberty, when she changed her name "to better reflect her Elven heritage." She has lived all her life in Seattle.

Having joined the Children only recently, she has less of an emotional connection with Templeman and Topal, and so may be more willing to listen to the runners' story.

Attributes

Body: 3
Quickness: 5
Strength: 2
Charisma: 6
Intelligence: 6
Willpower: 4
Essence: 6
Magic: 6
Reaction: 5

Skills

Conjuring: 5
Etiquette (Street): 4
Firearms: 3
Magical Theory: 3
Sorcery: 6
Unarmed Combat: 5

Dice Pools

Astral: 18
Defense (Armed): 1
Defense (Unarmed): 4
Dodge: 5
Magic: 6

Gear

Lined Coat (4/2)
Reusable Detection Fetish
Reusable Healing Fetish
Ruger Super Warhawk [6 (cyl), Laser Sights, 4M2]
Smoke Grenade
Thermographic Goggles

Spells

Detection:

Analyze Truth: 4
Detect Life: 4

Health:

Heal Moderate Wounds: 4
Heal Severe Wounds: 5

Manipulation:

Poltergeist: 4

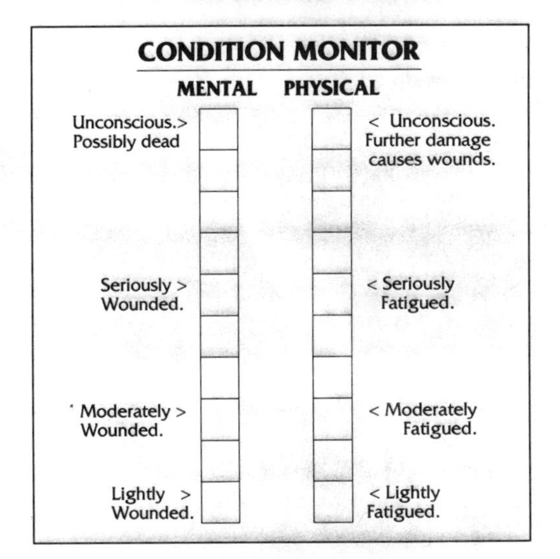

TELL IT TO THEM STRAIGHT

The contrast of going from the Redmond Barrens to this part of Tacoma is as abrupt as night suddenly turning into day. Within mere kilometers, excessive poverty gives way to material excess. Here, just north of the docks on the shore of Lake Washington, sits the gleaming black and silver metal of the Lochlann Center.

Approaching the building, you see no sign of guards. Nothing prevents you from entering the posh lobby of the Lochlann Center. It has been decorated to the hilt. Glass, marble, and real plants abound. A waterfall cascades from the third-floor atrium into a small pool to your left. Around you, wage slaves and corporate types stare at your rather unusual clothes. It's obvious they don't get many like you through the front door.

Across the lobby is a small reception desk. A sign on the front says "Information." You cross the room and greet the dutifully cheerful woman behind the plexiglass screen. She is all smiles, but nearly passes out when you ask to see Geyswain. Ashen-faced, she calls upstairs. You cannot hear the conversation, but the result is plain enough. The woman gestures you to an elevator that is almost hidden by the extensive foliage near the back wall. A single security man guards it.

As you amble over, the guard presses his hand to his ear and mumbles into his collar. By the time you reach him, the elevator door is open. The car's interior is paneled in teak wood, an expense that would be criminal were it not so beautiful. Once you are inside, the guard reaches in to press an unmarked button, then steps back quickly as the elevator door closes. You feel a rising sensation as the car speeds to the upper reaches of the building. The trip is brief, with no indication of how many levels you've ascended, but a good guess is that this is the top floor.

Entrance to Building

☐ = 25 meters

LOCHLANN ROOF

If a team member scouts astrally:

You're expecting resistance, some line of defense, but you find nothing. The building and the grounds around it are inert. Darting through the lower floors, you see plenty of late-night wage slaves, even a few security guards, but no sign of magic. You travel upward.

More building. More offices. Nothing. Finally, the top floors.

It's like entering another world. The upper three floors of the Lochlann Center have apparently been converted into a single open area, landscaped to resemble what you figure must be desert. You gaze around, absorbing the scene, when you hear a small cough from behind you. Turning slowly, you see the Dragon.

"Well, don't just hover there!" he says. "Go back to your body and then bring the rest of your friends up. I haven't got forever, you know!"

Entering Geyswain's lair:

When the door opens, the stinging smell of camphor assaults your senses. Your first breath is also a surprise as you suck in hot, dry air. Stepping out of the elevator, you see that this is an eco-center, an area designed to mimic a natural environment. Geyswain seems to like his lair hot and dry. You begin to perspire as the hot air wicks the moisture from your body.

The room itself is cavernous. Easily encompassing 2,000 square meters, it is as though you'd stepped into the Mojave Desert. Sandstone boulders are scattered about and full-sized flowering cactus provide color. If there are any windows, the rock outcroppings lining the walls hide them from view. You continue further into the room, feeling the hard-packed sand crunch beneath your feet. The elevator door closes behind you.

"Good afternoon, Humans. I am Geyswain." From behind a rock outcropping steps your host, a creature easily 20 meters long from snout to hind legs and with a tail of equal length. Spines ring his head and line the ridge of his back. His brown and red-scaled skin is covered with dark red plates. Approaching your group, he steps over several cacti, placing every foot with as much care as speed. As the Dragon walks, his tongue darts back and forth and his head weaves from side to side. Within seconds, he has crossed the room and is standing before you, his head a full two meters above yours. "Now, Humans, what is it you want to discuss?"

BEHIND THE SCENES

Before they can ascend to the Penthouse, the runners must leave their heavier weapons at the front desk. They can keep heavy pistols and anything lighter.

Upstairs, Geyswain listens carefully as the team makes their pitch. He has never seen, nor sensed, anything like the idol, but is familiar with occurrences of such phenomena. For him to examine it properly, it must be removed from the case and the magical barrier within. The Dragon will not handle the idol directly, but uses Levitate Item to bring it up to his eye level. He stares at it for a few moments, eyes slowly closing to slits. When done, he returns the object to its resting place.

If the team asks the Dragon to destroy the idol, Geyswain points out that the deed would require an arduous ritual on his part. Following his brief examination of the idol, he is actually eager to gain possession of the object, but he conceals this from the runners.

After the team finishes pleading their case, the Dragon appears to reflect for several moments, then agrees to attempt the destruction. Geyswain tells them that, unfortunately, the task will take some time and requires a closer examination of the idol to better orient his magic against it. The Dragon's main objective is to gain possession of the idol, and he will feign cooperation with the runners to get it. If any player-character magician asks to sit in on the ritual, Geyswain dismisses him with a snort, claiming that he must use "Dragon magic, which no mortal may view."

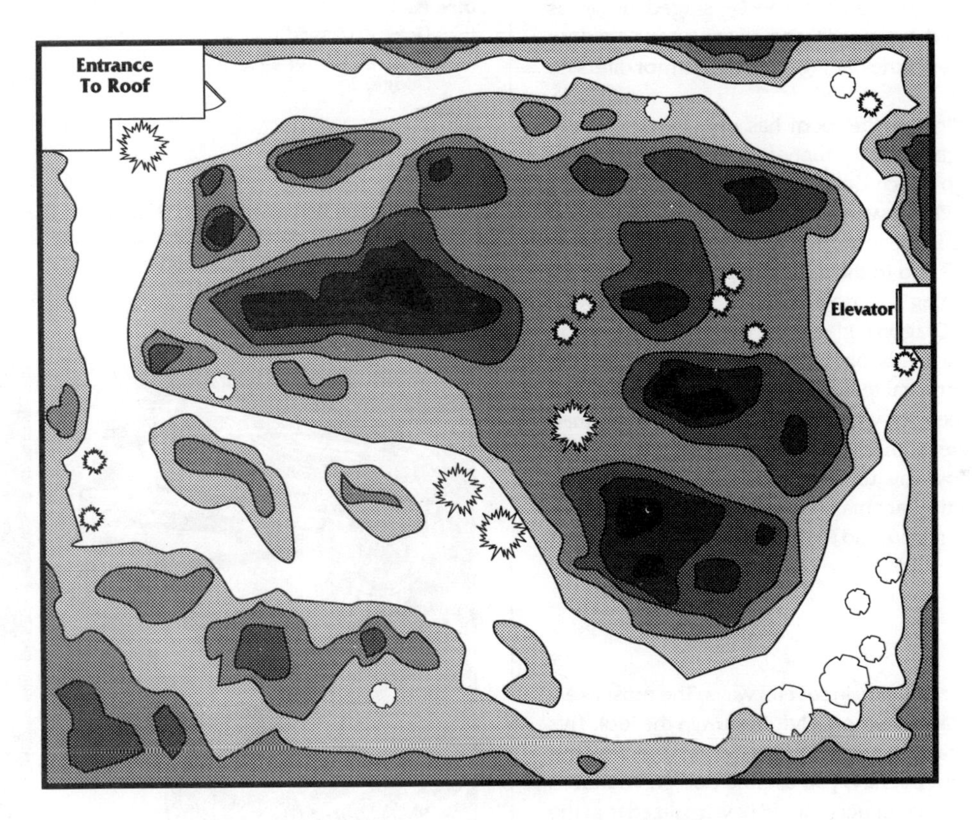

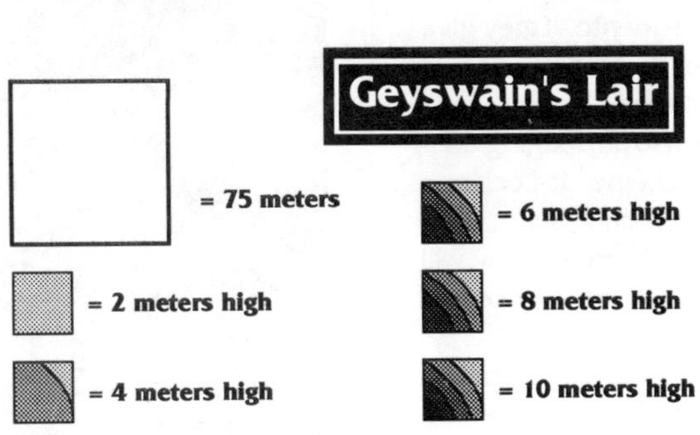

To maintain appearances, he bemoans the difficulty of performing the ritual and insists that he really should get something in return for his troubles. If the player characters have nothing of value to offer, Geyswain states that the team, as a group, now owes him a favor. The prospect of owing Geyswain a service is none too pleasing, but he will not accept less.

If the team is unwilling to surrender the idol, Geyswain asks them to wait a moment, then exits the room. His plan is to make the runners wait in this oven he calls a lair until they pass out from dehydration. When they are unconscious, Geyswain will call Medical to have the runners removed from the building, minus the idol. Each team member can stay in the room for 15 minutes before passing out. The initial conversation with the Dragon easily takes that much time.

For every minute after Geyswain leaves the room, each runner must make a Body Resistance Test against dehydration damage of 6S2 Fatigue. The gamemaster may wish to make the rolls himself to keep the players from being too suspicious. After they become Seriously Fatigued, however, the team begins to realize their dilemma. The damage can be staged down as normal damage. Add the Impact Rating of any armor a runner is wearing to the Power of the damage. Dermal Armor offers no protection.

As the map indicates, the room has only two exits: the elevator doors through which the runners entered and the large double doors through which Geyswain exited. Both are made of Reinforced Impact Plastic with a Barrier Rating of 20. Both are sealed. If the runners somehow open the elevator doors, they get access to the shaft and to the throng of guards (at least 20) waiting below. Opening the door through which Geyswain exited will reveal the Dragon curled up at the edge of a sloping ramp that apparently leads onto the roof. In this case, the Dragon hits the player characters with a full-strength, area-effect Sleep spell. If that does not work, he sends the waiting squad of security guards (eleven men) after the runners.

Regardless of how this turns out, the team will wake up several hours later at the Tacoma Charity Hospital, an establishment of questionable repute. Go to **Different Dragon**, the next section.

DEBUGGING

This section could develop in several ways. The most likely is that the player characters simply give Geyswain the idol. This probably means restraining any characters who have become "attached" to the item, but hey, you use the power, you takes your chances. By now, the runners should have realized that the idol is not something to keep around as a memento. If they give Geyswain the idol, he thanks them, reminds them that they owe him a service, and lets them leave unmolested.

If they will not give him the idol or seem to be hedging their bets, the Dragon uses his dehydration scheme. If Lochlann guards do get into the action, they will fire only Gel or Stun rounds from their weapons, under Geyswain's order. They will attempt to subdue the characters solely for the purpose of acquiring the idol.

Should the almost impossible occur and the player characters seem on the verge of defeating Geyswain and escaping with the idol, let them. Arleesh will find them soon enough.

LOCHLANN SECURITY GUARDS

The Human security guards will attempt to capture the runners if the team manages to flee Geyswain's lair. They will not use deadly force, at Geyswain's order. Once the runners are down, the guards will retrieve the idol and deliver the player characters to the hospital.

Attributes
- Body: 4
- Quickness: 3
- Strength: 3
- Charisma: 2
- Intelligence: 2
- Willpower: 2
- Essence: 6
- Reaction: 2

CONDITION MONITOR

	MENTAL	PHYSICAL	
Unconscious.> Possibly dead	☐	☐	< Unconscious. Further damage causes wounds.
	☐	☐	
	☐	☐	
	☐	☐	
Seriously > Wounded.	☐	☐	< Seriously Fatigued.
	☐	☐	
	☐	☐	
Moderately > Wounded.	☐	☐	< Moderately Fatigued.
	☐	☐	
Lightly > Wounded.	☐	☐	< Lightly Fatigued.

Skills
- Armed Combat: 3
- Etiquette (Corporate): 2
- Firearms: 3
- Interrogation: 2
- Unarmed Combat: 3

Dice Pools
- Defense (Armed): 3
- Defense (Unarmed): 3
- Dodge: 3

Gear
- Earplug Radio
- Helmet (1/1)
- Plastic Restraints
- Remington Roomsweeper [6 (Magazine), 12 extra rounds, Laser Sight, 3M3 normal, 4L1 Stun Gel round]
- Stun Baton (+ 1 Reach, 5L2 Stun + Special)
- Vest with Plates (4/3)

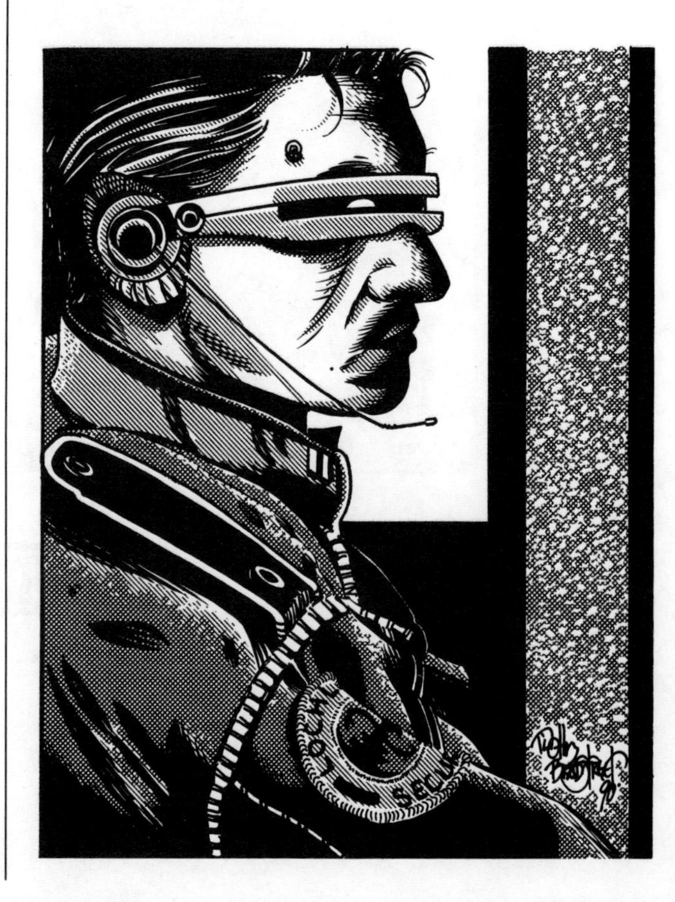

DIFFERENT DRAGON

TELL IT TO THEM STRAIGHT

If the runners get roughed up by Geyswain:

You've been here at least 24 hours, which means your credstick's probably crashed. What's more, the woman in the next bed looks to be dying from some highly communicable disease, and there's a guy down the hall who keeps screaming something about bugs, no matter how much tranquilizer they pump into him.

The doctors' plastic smiles match their clothes as they congratulate you on your speedy recovery. They want you to pass on their regards to the magician who healed you, which confuses you even more. A quick check with the magicians in your group confirms that none of them did it.

Anyway, except for your tongues feeling like fur, you feel fine, and the hospital wants to use your beds for some other runners who just lost an argument with Aztechnology. The staff hands you the sealed safety bags containing your gear. You search them quickly, and sure enough, no idol. Ah well.

Out the front door and you are greeted with a rare sight: a sunny day and a beautiful woman. Leaning against a long, sleek, white Mitsubishi Nightsky, she wears mirrorshades that catch your reflections. With a rueful shake of the head, she smiles thinly.

"You know," she says, "somebody really should teach you the differences between Dragons."

If the team walked away from Lochlann:

Well, you may be rid of the idol, but your troubles are far from over. Your friends and contacts still treat you like lepers, word on the street is that you're a bunch of cowards who killed their employer for 50 nuyen, and any squatter will still run for the nearest vidphone when you walk by. And then there's Lone Star.

Speaking of Lone Star, you suddenly notice a pair of Lone Star cruisers doing the slow crawl nearby. Bad sign. You duck into a nearby alley, where you catch a glimpse of another cruiser passing at the other end. You're starting to think about going to the roofs when another car pulls into the alley.

You turn, guns ready, but it's a long, sleek, white Mitsubishi Nightsky. The driver's door opens and a beautiful woman wearing an earth-toned headdress steps out. She looks you over, lifts the mirrorshades from her eyes, and scowls. "Well, are you just going to stand there and get arrested, or are you going to get into the car?" she asks.

You scramble to pile in. As the woman pulls clear of the alley and the patrol cars, she glances back at you all. "Good, now that you're all here, I think it's time somebody taught you the difference between Dragons."

BEHIND THE SCENES

Any player character who is under the idol's influence (see **Playing With Darkness**) will not be in the best of health following the runner's brief stay in the hospital. He is still suffering any physical, mental, or mystical effects caused by separation from the idol.

Arleesh, as the woman eventually identifies herself, quickly examines the depleted runner or runners, then scowls some more. "You really shouldn't play with things you don't understand," she says. "There's nothing I can do, but you'll probably be fine in a few days or so. You were lucky."

She drives the Nightsky to a local Stuffer Shack drive-through, gets what everybody wants, and then parks nearby. If one of the magicians present slips into Astral Space and assenses Arleesh while she's driving, he immediately discovers that she is a Great Feathered Serpent. If no magician makes the attempt, the first thing she says after parking the Nightsky is, "Assense me. I will allow you to see my real form."

After her identity has been confirmed, she explains:

"My name is Arleesh. I am a Great Feathered Serpent of ancient and honorable lineage. Until the other night, you had in your possession an artifact of great power, a vessel of corruption. The Dog shaman with whom you spoke was correct in saying that only a Dragon has the wisdom to destroy the vessel, but unfortunately, her knowledge of Dragons is as limited as yours. Yes, I've spoken with her.

"Geyswain is what, in your language, is known as a Dracoform. A more suitable term might be *Lesser Dragon*, however, as opposed to my type, which humans term a *Great Dragon*. But no matter. The point is that you gave the object to the wrong Dragon. Even now, Geyswain is attempting to learn the secrets of the idol and to harness its power. That must not happen.

"As this is partly your fault, you must assist me in stopping Geyswain. If he should tap the secrets of that object, it could cause an irrevocable shift in the natural order. I intend to attack him in his lair, and you must come with me."

Arleesh will not accept any refusal from the runners. She points out that if any other Great Dragons learn of what they have done...well, the player characters can figure it out from there. She tells them to meet her on the Tacoma docks at 1:00 A.M. that night. From there, they will make their way to Lochlann. She suggests that they rest, plan, and get as much firepower as they think they'll need. She then drives them to wherever they wish to go. Within reason, of course.

DEBUGGING

Well, the runners can say no to Arleesh if they wish. Or if they decide not to show up at the docks, she goes after Geyswain by herself. The next day, the runners will hear of a terrible fire at Lochlann and that the body of a Dragon was found. The gamemaster should determine whose body it is, whether that of Geyswain or Arleesh.

If it is Geyswain's, the runners can surmise that Arleesh was victorious and has probably destroyed the idol. Now all they have to worry about is her retribution.

If it is Arleesh's, that is even worse news. Was Arleesh right about Geyswain unleashing terrible horrors on the world if he learns the secret of the idol? And what will happen when the Dragon realizes that the only others who know the truth about what's going on are the runners?

Like Arleesh said, they should rest, plan, and grab as much firepower as they can. It's gonna be a hot time in the old town tonight.

TELL IT TO THEM STRAIGHT

Fortunately, the lone white Nightsky doesn't look too out of place in front of the abandoned storefront. You enter and find Arleesh inside, decked out in a long, white leather evening dress with front and back plunges and a side-slit that nearly meet in the same place. She smiles as you enter. "No, we're not going to a party," she says. "It's all part of the plan."

If a player-character decker is present:

Arleesh motions to a nearby wall section, where you see panels ripped away to expose the telecom lines. It's a simple matter to patch in your deck and start skating. The Lochlann construct is nearby, sitting on the edge of a neon void that symbolically marks the edge of Lake Washington. You eye its series of interlinked geodesic shapes and then move closer.

After moving carefully to within sensor range, you bring the appropriate programs on line. The results scroll through your mind's eye, but you can't believe them. But when you run the programs again, the same results appear. Nothing. Nada. The construct's there, the pathways are there, but there's no security. Nothing to block the SAN. This is either real good, or very, very bad. With no little trepidation, you begin to move forward. This is, after all, a Dragon's lair.

The SAN is cold, and it takes little more than a flick of the wrist to get through. Too easy, you think. As an amber pathway opens up ahead, you pause to check out the SAN more thoroughly. There's IC there, all right, but it's dead. The systems are present, but there's nothing commanding them.

You slide further into the system, through the amber tunnel, and move into the heart of the Lochlann Matrix. It's only a few short turns to the CPU, again with nothing blocking your way. One glance at the central processor tells you all you need to know: this system's been burned.

If the decker is a non-player character:

The decker nods once at you, runs his fingers through his short red hair, and jacks in. He whistles as his fingers fly over the deck's simple command board, augmenting his cybernetic control.

"Hmm," he says after a moment. "I've got the Lochlann 'struct, quad-linked geodesics shifting from emerald to sapphire in a sinosodial pattern. Mid-sized. Fairly rough imagery. Either a slip and slide or trash and crash. Time to...well, that's oddo."

"What?" says Arleesh, leaning in closer.

"SAN's a blank. Squatto."

"It's sealed?"

"Noper. It's clean-squeak open. No sign of IC anywhere."

"Well, that's odd. Isn't it?"

"That's what I peeped before, righto?"

"Um, yes."

"Anyway, let me do a little hunt and peck in here..." His fingers flash again. "Yupper. Quiet as a corpse. I'm gonna penetrate."

You watch in silence as he whistles and occasionally grunts, his blanked-out eyes locked onto a point on the far wall. "Crash and burn, chummers. The CPU's just about gone to quantum heaven," he says suddenly. "Somebody's roasted the puppy but fine."

Arleesh frowns. "Someone got in before you?"

He grins. "Noper. This one's an inside job. When I say burn, I mean burn. We're talking physical damage to the CPU."

"Well, that's not good," Arleesh says. "We'd better get over there." She hands one of you a small gym bag and tells you to hold it until everyone is inside Lochlann. Arleesh mumbles half to herself, "Look's like there's going to be a party after all," and you all rush out onto the street.

When the runners arrive at Lochlann:

It's quiet, dead quiet. There's no visible sign of activity either on the grounds around the building or in the lobby. Odd thing is, most of the building's lights seem to be on.

As you watch the building, a cool wind blows in off the lake, followed within moments by the first hint of rain. It's going to be a dark night.

If a runner scouts Lochlann astrally:

In sharp contrast to the physical scene at Lochlann, the astral realm immediately around the building is teeming with activity. From a distance, you can easily see dozens of elementals and spirits careening madly around the upper floors of the building, either protecting some unknown perimeter or orbiting some unseen central point.

You drift closer and realize that it would be foolish to attempt to enter. Something about these spirits isn't right. They seem as interested in tearing into each other as anything else.

BEHIND THE SCENES

If the decker is a non-player character, then his job is done and he will depart into the night, after receiving suitable payment from Arleesh. If the decker is a player character, he's along for the rest of the ride.

The plan is for the runners to position themselves near the main entrance to Lochlann. At a prearranged moment, the decker is to confuse the Lochlann system while Arleesh, decked out in her killer evening clothes, dashes through the pouring rain and into the lobby. She will play the "help me, I am a poor, helpless, incredibly good-looking, rainsoaked lady with car trouble" bit to the hilt, then take out the guards there. It should all have been so simple.

The runners move into position, Arleesh drives up and stalls the car in front of the lobby, dashes through the downpour into the lobby, and stops dead. It's empty. After gesturing the rest of the team inside, she points out that the security cameras also look to be inactive.

A quick look around the lobby reveals two dead bodies. One, apparently the security guard, is behind the reception desk. He looks as though he's been dead for years. The guard's gun is only a meter or so away from him, and if the runners examine it, they will see that it has been fired recently.

What must have been the dead guard's target is the other body, lying by the elevators. This fellow is in much the same condition as the first guard, except that he's got five bullets in him.

Arleesh insists that the runners head down to the basement, where her information locates the Security Center. If anyone protests, she points out the inconvenience of having a horde of guards suddenly show up to ambush them just as she and the team are making their move against Geyswain. She adds that a look at the Security Center might help them get an idea of what's going on in the rest of the building. After telling the team to meet her up in Geyswain's lair when they're done, Arleesh takes her gym bag from the player character who's been holding it, then heads for the upper floors.

If any runners attempt to follow her, they will find her waiting—and scowling—just around the next turn of the corridor. No matter what they say, Arleesh claims that she must be alone to prepare for her meeting with Geyswain. Nothing can persuade her otherwise.

To get down to the Security Center, the runners can use either the stairs or the elevator. If they call an elevator, it appears, but is full of the torn and mangled dead bodies of wage slaves. It looks as though they killed each other. Though the elevator car is full of bodies, all with the same long-dead appearance, it is still operable.

The stairs are free of bodies, but an ominous stain marks the last landing before the basement level.

When the runners reach the basement, everything looks normal. But only at first.

SECURITY CENTER MAP KEY

Corridors

The corridors of the basement are monitored by security cameras that feed images directly into the subprocessor. A security technician/computer operator normally watches as the computer selects a camera to feed to one of the monitors in the control room. If desired, the operator can manually switch the feed to any monitor. At the moment, however, none of the cameras seem to be working.

Locker Room

While on duty, the guards store their belongings in these rows of lockers. When off-duty, they use the lockers to store their uniforms and equipment. The room is also equipped with showers. The two doors are always unlocked. The room is currently in a state of disarray. If the runners search it, they will discover a man's mauled form along the wall. The marks on his body weren't made by an animal, however. They could only have been made by a Human.

Briefing Room

This room is set up like a classroom, with a small stage and podium up front. A dry-erase board on the front wall shows the names and appointed locations of all guards for the shift as well as notices and special reports. According to the information, this shift had four people in the basement, plus six other guards in the building, not counting Geyswain's residence on the top floor. The two doors to this room are always kept unlocked.

Break Room

Chester, the shift supervisor, is in the break room when the team first enters the basement. He remains there until the runners discover him, at which time he attacks them. Chester is insane, homicidally deranged. Nothing the runners do can help him. Use the **Lochlann Security Guard** stats given later in this section. Chester attacks with his bare hands.

Shift Supervisor's Office

The three shift supervisors use this office. Each has his own desk, locker, and computer console. Dry-erase boards line the walls. Each board is covered with cryptic messages and reminders. Two of the desks are littered messes, but the third is spotlessly clean. This room is usually occupied at all times, but Chester, the supervisor for the third shift, is off getting a midnight snack. The door to the hallway is always unlocked. The door to the computer room is locked with a Maglock (6), activated by a palm scanner to the right of the door.

Security Administration

Four secretaries work during the first shift in this office. The room is locked, Maglock (5) with palm scanner, for the night.

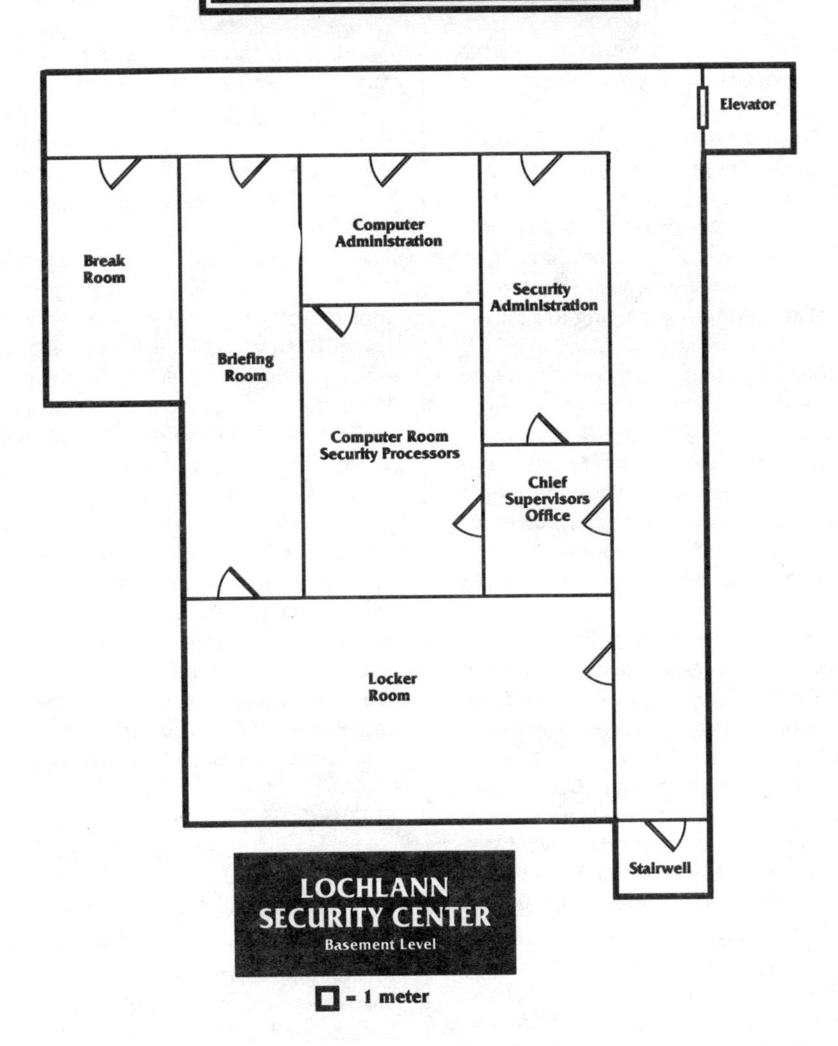

Computer Administration Office

One Company Man and one secretary share this office during the day. They are responsible for overseeing the work and activities of the 15-man crew that operates the security subprocessor. Inside are two desks, each with a computer. The room is currently locked, Maglock (5) with palm scanner, for the night.

Computer Room

This room is the heart of Lochlann's automated security system. Inside, three technicians are supposed to man the computers 24 hours a day. One is jacked into the Matrix, one handles incoming external security processing, and the third watches the local security monitors. The room is protected by PANICBUTTONS at each work station, and these will seal the room and sound the alarm when pressed. A pressure-sensitive plate hooked into the alarm system is located in front of the main door. The plate activates at 5:00 P.M., when the Computer Administrator leaves for the day. If the technicians leave during the night, they exit through the shift supervisor's office. Each of the doors to the computer room is locked, Maglock (6) with palm scanner, at all times.

At the moment, only one living technician is in the room. Seated calmly in one corner, he is devouring the remaining bits and pieces of his two co-workers. When the runners arrive, he barely acknowledges their presence.

The computers in the room are security processors, all physically damaged beyond repair as a result of the fight that took place here.

Eventually, the runners leave the basement and make their way up to the penthouse to meet Arleesh and Geyswain. If they take the time to search any of the rest of the building, they will find evidence of extensive violence, but no bodies.

Reaching the penthouse, the runners enter through the same double doors as before. This time, however, they do not encounter the dry heat of the environmentally controlled penthouse. Rather, the air is cool and moist, with a slight breeze. Perhaps from an opening somewhere?

The lights are dim, as though the area had been set for night, but the runners can still make out, in the first major clearing, a pile of bodies as high as they are. The stench is almost unbearable, with each body looking as though it had been lying here for days.

Just beyond them, crouched in the near-dark, is Geyswain. As the runners approach, the Dragon lets out a low growl and tosses aside the "flesh toy" he had been playing with. "Ah," he says, "perhaps your blood will be strong enough." The runners are startled to see the figure of of the "flesh toy" suddenly roll to its feet and stagger toward them. As the person passes through the area of light, the player characters recognize him as Bloodwing. He and the rest of his team tracked the runners to

Lochlann earlier and guessed that the team must have left the idol there. A few hours ago, they entered, hoping to recover the object, only to be trounced by the Dragon.

Without further ado, Geyswain launches himself forward at the runners. As he, too, moves through the area of light, the player characters can see that the Dragon's body has suffered horrible deterioration. Enormous, puss-filled sores cover his form, and his scales are cracking and sliding from him. Tears have appeared in his wings. None of this concerns Geyswain, however. He flings himself at the runners, bringing to bear the full might of his power.

Bloodwing will be more than willing to lend a hand against the Dragon if the team provides him with a weapon.

Arleesh is nowhere to be seen at first. She is actually close by, but cloaked in an Invisibility spell, waiting for the runners to wear down Geyswain. It is her plan to sacrifice the player characters to the Dragon while she holds back her power for eventual use against the idol. She cannot afford to become injured in battle with Geyswain, and then be too weakened to destroy the idol.

Once Geyswain is Seriously Wounded, he will make a hasty retreat, attempting to escape via the roof. If able to reach the roof, he can fly away and hide in the low storm-cloud cover. His plan does not take account of one thing, however, and that is Lone Star.

In the past 24 hours, the events at Lochlann Center have become too big to ignore. After receiving a report that the runners had been seen near there, Grissim posted a surveillance team in the area. He also knows that 60 percent of the Lochlann work force didn't come home for dinner that evening. He has also been informed of the odd goings-on in astral space in the vicinity of the building. Putting two and two together, and adding in the rumors about some crazy stone idol and the involvement of certain powerful figures from Tir Tairngire, the Captain figured this was going to be where the gauna hit the rotating blades. That is the reason he brought in a huge number of Lone Star troops to cordon off the building. He also ordered some troopers to land on the roof, ready to deal with whatever comes out of Lochlann.

When Geyswain reaches the roof, he runs into a dozen or so heavily armed Lone Star troopers and a handful of circling Wasp and Yellowjacket helicopters. Also circling a short distance away is an Ares Dragon transport helicopter configured as Grissim's command post. Geyswain takes one look at the firepower up here before screaming in anger and rushing back at the player characters, determined to take them with him.

He does not know that Lone Star will not get involved. This is private property, after all. Unless the fight spills over into the surrounding neighborhood, Grissim's Lone Star troops will not fire a single shot for or against the runners. The Captain will just sit back and watch.

Eventually, Geyswain will be able to fight no more. Once that occurs, Arleesh will appear in her true form as a Great Feathered Serpent and tear the idol from Geyswain's grasp. The runners and Lone Star watch as the idol levitates before her, begins to spin wildly about both its axes, turning into a glowing blue-purple ball of energy, and then going dark in a tremendous implosion of light and sound.

In the stunned silence that follows, Arleesh, the incredible strain evident even on her powerful body, flips the now-inert idol to one of the runners. "Here," she calls. "Have fun. And thanks." That's the last they hear as she flies off, passing ominously close to Grissim's chopper.

As soon as Arleesh has disappeared into the cloud cover, Grissim orders his chopper down onto the roof, where he all but leaps out to get to the player characters.

If Bloodwing is still alive, he immediately demands the idol, claiming it as stolen property of Tir Tairngire. Not being a mage, Bloodwing has no idea of what the idol might be, and so does not understand what Arleesh did to it. All he knows is that his instructions were to get the idol and return it to Tir Tairngire.

Odds are that the runners will give the idol to Bloodwing. Unless they want it as a gruesome memento, they have no reason to hold onto it now. He will offer them 50,000 nuyen, non-negotiable, for the idol.

Just as Bloodwing and the runners are working out a deal, Grissim comes running over. He pulls his Predator and holds it to Bloodwing's head, arresting him in the name of Lone Star and the people of Seattle. In response, Bloodwing flashes a smile, reaches into a back pocket, and produces a diplomatic pass. It identifies him as an Associate Ambassador to Tir Tairngire and, therefore, diplomatically immune.

Grissim is definitely not pleased.

DEBUGGING

The most important, and difficult, aspect of this section is managing the conflict between Geyswain and the runners. It is intended that this be a knock-down, drag-out fight between the runners and Geyswain, but only if the preceding events and the characters present make that logical. The gamemaster must keep several things in mind.

•If Geyswain is losing too easily, remember the numerous rogue elementals and spirits floating around his lair. They are more than willing to be sacrificed in his favor. Assume that the spirits are all Force 3 and that Geyswain has access to one or two at any given moment.

•If the player characters need more firepower, Bloodwing, and possibly Harper and Tundra, are lurking nearby, having narrowly escaped Geyswain's wrath. If things get really bad, Children of Sophocles members could appear on the scene to lend a hand.

The gamemaster can handle the resolution of the adventure as he wishes. After Grissim witnesses the climax of the battle with Geyswain, it will not be hard to persuade Grissim that the runners are not involved with Bloodwing. Grissim will be furious that Bloodwing has diplomatic immunity, which the Elf will produce, regardless of whether he gets the idol.

As for the idol, if Bloodwing gets it, he returns it to Tir Tairngire. He will have to explain to his masters why it no longer has its former magical powers, but that will still be the end of the evil object.

If the idol does not go to Tir Tairngire, then somebody else has it. Who? And how long before someone else comes looking for it?

CONTACTS

At some point during the adventure, the runners should attempt to use their Contacts to find out what is going on. When they do, consult the appropriate sections below. The information is presented in the order that the player characters are likely to encounter it.

LONE STAR

The heat has come down so heavy that everybody on the streets knows that Lone Star wants the runners, bad. Lone Star cops have made a visit everywhere the runners are known, rousting friends and acquaintances and hassling even those who are only passing acquaintances. Friendship only goes so far.

Appropriate Contacts (Target Number 5)

Any Non-Corporate Contact or any non-Lone Star Law Enforcement Contact

HEAT IS ON

Successes	Result
0	"What, are you stupid, chummer? You've boned it, really boned it. Get outta my face!" (If this is a meeting in person, this Contact might turn the runners over to Lone Star, depending on his past history with the team.)
1 – 2	"Wizzer, son, what did you do? Lone Star's everywhere, hassling everybody. One of their Captains, a buzz-head named Grissim, is callin' the shots."
3 – 4	"Man, you are so hot I could roast weenies on your shadow. I think you were just plain in the wrong place at the wrong time, and now Lone Star's connected you up with somebody."
5+	"Geez, waddaya doin, callin me here? If they got my phone tapped, I'll geek ya. I swear! Look, I don't know how you got involved with that Bloodwing joker, but I don't wanna hear from you no more."

The following is available if the runners have a direct contact with Lone Star (Target 7).

HOTLINE

Successes	Result
0	The Contact refuses to speak with the runner.
1 – 2	"Look, you've got to turn yourself in. There's stuff going on here you just don't understand. The bosses upstairs want Bloodwing bad, and that means they want you."
3 – 4	"You shouldn't have called me. Lord knows who might be listening. Look, the board of directors is getting leaned on heavy by somebody. I don't know who, but that's why they're leaning on you."
5+	"Geez, you really don't know how to do things half-way, do you? Any idea who we have upstairs right now? An ambassador from Tir Tairngire. Do you understand what that means?"

CAPTAIN GRISSIM

Grissim is in many ways the archetypal iron-jawed Lone Star trooper, and he knows it. He is, however, one of the most straight-shooting cops on the beat. Sure he has a temper and a long-memory, but he's not stupid.

He wants Bloodwing from his days with Lone Star-LA when a rash of political killings in that town were attributed to the Elven hitman. As the head of that investigation, Grissim was unable to pin anything on Bloodwing, which is how he got transferred to Seattle.

Appropriate Contacts (Target 6)

Any Street or Law Enforcement-related Contact

OLD IRON-JAW

Successes	Result
0	No Result
1 – 2	"Grissim? Gawd, the guy's after your butt and you're asking me about *him*? Why don't you just give him a call? I'm sure the Lone Star switchboard will connect you. With the company you keep, it's no wonder he's after you."
3 – 4	"That guy's one tough trooper, I'll tell ya. But there's one thing I gotta give him. He's as straight as they come. If he gives his word, you can count on it."
5+	"Grissim? Chummer, Grissim doesn't want you. He wants Bloodwing, and like it or not, you're connected to that damned Elf. The only way you're gonna get Grissim off your back is to give him Bloodwing."

BLOODWING

Bloodwing. Speak that name in some circles and you'll see expressions of either fear or respect. One-half of the infamous Bloodwing-Nightprince team of Elven assassins, he has been attributed a perfect record of 37 confirmed terminations. What this cool, calculating killer lacks in the spontaneity of his teammate, he more than makes up for in professionalism.

Hired by an unnamed Tir Tairngire noble, Bloodwing's job is to get the idol, but not to make any noise doing it. Unfortunately, unforeseen events have driven him underground.

He's keeping his eyes and ears open, waiting for the runners and the idol to surface.

Appropriate Contacts (Target 8)

Any Law Enforcement Contact, any Elven contact, any Hitman or Mercenary Contact

ELVEN HITMAN

Successes	Result
0	No result
1 – 2	"Bloodwing? Yes, I have heard of him. Are you involved with him somehow? What kind of flowers would you like?"
3 – 4	"If he has agreed to do something, he will do it. There is no dissuading him. I hear he's in town after something, but I don't know what it is."
5+	"Swear you won't tell anybody I told you this, O.K.? I mean, like, I'd be dead if you did, O.K.? One of the big mucky-mucks from Elfland hired him. Whatever it is they want, they want it bad."

TOPAL

All that can be learned about Topal is some ultimately pointless information about his life. Maybe, however, the runners will get lucky.

Appropriate Contacts (Target 10)

Any Magical Contact

MR. JOHNSON

Successes	Result
0	No result
1 – 2	"Yeah, I hearda him. Ran a talismonger shop called The Guided Hand, didn't he? Place burned down a night or two ago."
3 – 4	"Raven shaman, right? Real fat pig of a man, if it's who I think he is. Got some back-room club that he hangs with. Children of...of...gawd, some philosopher guy or something..."
5+	"Yes, he's a member of the Children of Sophocles, if I'm not mistaken. Armchair magicians. I think one of their people just died. Guy named Templeman, Simon Templeman."

CHILDREN OF SOPHOCLES

People on the street don't take the Children of Sophocles seriously, calling them armchair magicians because they've got little direction or purpose. Founded by Simon Templeman as a true scholarly society, the Children have lately degenerated into little more than a social club.

Appropriate Contacts (Target 6)

Any Magical Contact

ARMCHAIR MAGICIANS

Successes	Result
0	No result
1 – 2	"The who? Oh, you mean The Kids? Yeah, right. Buncha tarot-card-turning idiots, if you ask me. Couldn't call up a first-rank quasi-elemental, if ya ask me."
3 – 4	"Yeah, that's the group that Simon Templeman used to run with in Sophocles, isn't it? Poor guy. Hear he caught some rare South Pacific disease on his last trip. Poor guy."
5+	"Chummer, those jokers are gunning for you! I swear, I heard 'em talking. They want you for geeking Topal, and they think maybe you had something to do with Templeman buying it. Waddaya mean you didn't do Topal? Yeah, right...Sure."

SIMON TEMPLEMAN

Well-known and somewhat respected, Templeman has always been viewed as a bit eccentric. A multi-discipline scholar, he might shift focus at a moment's notice to dash off in pursuit of some new interest. The Children of Sophocles were one such interest, until something else distracted him. Whenever Templeman was off doing something else, Topal was the ad-hoc leader.

Appropriate Contacts (Target 8)

Any Magical Contact

DEAD MAN OUT

Successes	Results
0	No Result
1 – 2	"Sure ise hearda Templeman. Mage-guy that ran da Children of Sophocles, right?"
3 – 4	"Ah yes, Simon Templeman. Now there was a fellow. Last I heard, he was digging up ancient civilizations somewhere in the South Pacific."
5+	"Templeman? Yes, they cremated him last week. Poor fellow, I hear he looked like hell when he died. Must have caught something in the South Pacific."

THE IDOL

Research into the history of the idol ends with Simon Templeman because no one knows where he found it, except that it may have been somewhere in the South Pacific.

For more information on the idol, see **Playing With Darkness**, p. 51.

If the team shows the idol to a Magical Contact who has Magical Theory Skill, they may obtain some additional information.

Appropriate Contact (Target 4)

Any Magical Contact (with Magical Theory)

MYSTERIOUS POWER

Successes	Result
0	No result
1 – 2	"Hey, pretty cool. Power focus of some kind? Really neat. Hey! How come I can use it? How come you can use it?"
3 – 4	"Um...this is very strange. I have never seen anything like it. But come to think of it, someone's been asking about a thing that looks like this. She's a two-bit fortune teller out in the Barrens. Lady by the name of Trixy."
5+	"Chummer, I don't know what you got or where you got it, but I don't like it. Kinda gives me the chillies, ya dig?"

GEYSWAIN

Arrived in Seattle some 12 twelve years ago, Geyswain surprised people by going into real estate in the Barrens. Spurred on by the Dragon's capital, Lochlann Investments quickly became a major player in local real estate. Observers have noted, however, that most of Geyswain's acquisitions remain off the market and undeveloped. Perhaps he knows something they don't?

Appropriate Contacts (Target 5)

Any Corporate or Financial Contact

A LESSER DRAGON

Successes	Results
0	No result
1 – 2	"Yes, an interesting fellow. Good, solid business sense but occasionally partakes in, shall we say, some rather draconian practices?"
3 – 4	"Arrogant bugger, ain't he? Always knows best."
5+	"You'll note he's got a rather large scar on his left flank. I hear he got it during a, um, hostile takeover in Aztlan."

STREET RUMORS

Lots can be learned on the streets, even though most of the runners' contacts do not want to talk to them. Whenever a player character goes out to make a contact or learn some information, have him make an Etiquette (Street) Test, Target Number 4, to learn any of the following information.

WORD IS OUT

Successes	Results
0	No result
1	"I can't believe the heat that's coming down these days. You can't breathe without some Star busting your butt. What did these jokers do?"
2	"Somebody's pushing Lone Star's buttons on this. I ain't seen them so bent since what's-his-face was going around AVMing the monorail."
3	"Boy, those chummers are really bad news. Everybody's looking for them. One of 'em was a real great looker who came in wearing some kind of fancy headdress and asking after them. Don't know who she was, but she snapped Sammy's fingers when he got too feelie, if ya know what I mean."
4	"Yeah, I hears that Tir Tairngire's involved somehow. Seems that somebody on their hit list is in town and they want Lone Star to get him real bad."
5+	"Geez, yeah, somebody told me the Tir's sent in a bunch of Paladins to take care of the runners. Can you believe it? Paladins! Gawd, I feel sorry for those chummers."

CORPORATE

The only corporate information that might be pertinent to this adventure concerns Lochlann Investments.

LOCHLANN INVESTMENTS

Home Office: Tacoma, Seattle
President/CEO: Geyswain
Principal Divisions:
Division Name: Lochlann Real Estate
Division Head: Geyswain
Chief Products/Services: Local real estate acquisition and management corporation. Extensive holdings in Redmond, Puyallup, and Tacoma.

Business Profile:

This decade-old company is owned and administered by the low-profile Western Dragon Geyswain. Rarely seen outside his ecologically engineered living quarters on the top floors of the Lochlann Center in Tacoma, just north of the docks, he is nonetheless an active part of the corporation. Unlike the few other Dragons who run corporations, Geyswain seems to keep a claw in the daily activities of the corporation.

Though Lochlann has extensive real estate holdings, very little ever shows up for redevelopment or resale.

Security/Military Forces:

Lochlann maintains its own internal, moderate-strength security force. Their security personnel periodically receive retraining at the local Knight Errant training facility.

CAST OF CHARACTERS

NON-PLAYER CHARACTERS

The following NPCs play principal roles in the story of **Bottled Demon.** Because they will likely appear more than once in the course of the adventure, their statistics and descriptions are grouped together here for convenience. Descriptions and statistics for other, minor characters appear in the section of **The Adventure** where they make their appearance.

GEYSWAIN

Geyswain is fairly normal for a Western Dragon. He awakened in the deserts of the American Southwest almost 20 years ago and has since traveled over most of the Western Hemisphere, observing and then moving on. After visiting Seattle, he realized the potential long-term value of the land in the Barrens, especially to one as long-lived as him, and used some of his hidden hoard to buy land.

Geyswain has two major flaws. He is arrogant and he is very young. This deadly combination has given him many problems in the past, but this time, matters are much more serious. Geyswain knows something of the forces that power the idol, but he has never experienced them first-hand. Thus is he ignorant of the danger it represents. If he were a little wiser, he would know to destroy the item outright. If he were a little more powerful, and a Great Dragon, he actually could. Because he is neither, the idol's power will consume Geyswain unless something intervenes. Geyswain is not really evil or stupid; he just doesn't understand the long-term consequences of his actions.

For all his size and age, Geyswain is like a child. He is arrogant, even for a Dragon, and consistently fails to learn from his many mistakes. Even when his errors are pointed out, Geyswain can explain them away. It is this cockiness that makes Geyswain something of an outsider, even among other Dracoforms.

He considers the scar on his flank a badge of courage, proof that he can take it as well as dish it out. Most others would consider it proof of a foolish mistake.

Attributes
- Body: 14 (6)
- Quickness: 7 x 3
- Strength: 40
- Charisma: 3
- Intelligence: 5
- Willpower: 8
- Essence: 8
- Magic: 8
- Reaction: 6

Dice Pools
- Astral: 22
- Dodge: 7
- Magic: 9

Attack Code
- 10D3
- +2 Reach

Powers
- Low-Light Eyes
- Noxious Breath (10S2)
- Wide Band Hearing

Skills
- Conjuring: 7
- Etiquette (Corporate): 5
- Magical Theory: 8
- Sorcery: 9

Special Skills
- Finance: 7
- Language (English): 8

CONDITION MONITOR

MENTAL		PHYSICAL	
Unconscious.> Possibly dead	☐	☐	< Unconscious. Further damage causes wounds.
	☐	☐	
	☐	☐	
	☐	☐	
Seriously > Wounded.	☐	☐	< Seriously Fatigued.
	☐	☐	
	☐	☐	
Moderately > Wounded.	☐	☐	< Moderately Fatigued.
	☐	☐	
Lightly > Wounded.	☐	☐	< Lightly Fatigued.

Spells

Combat:
- Hellblast: 7
- Manaball: 12
- Mana Dart: 10
- Power Bolt: 8
- Sleep: 10

Detection:
- Clairvoyance: 8
- Detect Enemies: 7
- Detect Life: 8

Health:
- Detox Deadly Toxin: 7
- Heal Severe Wounds: 8

Illusion:
- Confusion: 6
- Invisibility: 8
- Stink: 8

Manipulation:
- Armor: 8
- Ignite: 8
- Levitate Item: 8
- Magic Fingers: 10
- Toxic Wave: 6

GRISSIM

Grissim has made a solid reputation for himself in his nearly 20 years of service to Seattle and Lone Star. His record is spotless and his unofficial influence spreads to nearly every part of Lone Star's operations. Though he has never risen above the rank of Captain, he is the idol of many of the city's street cops. Tough, but fair, he commands squads with some of the best arrest records in the city.

Grissim is an iron-jawed, blue-eyed rock of a man. His once-dark hair has begun to gray at the temples, but that only adds to his good looks. He keeps his uniform spotless, creased, and in perfect condition. When on a run, he can blend in with the local populace, mimicking perfectly the local customs and habits.

Though Grissim has an extensive set of dermal plates, no one recognizes it. The Swedish implants are so carefully placed as to appear completely natural.

Working with Grissim can be tough, for he demands a person's best at all times, under all conditions. He has also been known to strike a subordinate at times, to punctuate his orders. Living by the same rules he imposes on others, the Captain would never send an officer into a situation he would not face himself. For that reason, he often takes personal command of dangerous raids.

Grissim is concerned about the law, but he is more concerned with justice. His long years on the force have taught him that sometimes he must go with his instincts and do what feels right.

Grissim is loyal to Lone Star and all the men and women who serve it. He is also loyal to the city of Seattle and its inhabitants. He would gladly risk his life in the line of duty.

Attributes
- Body: 6 (8)
- Quickness: 4
- Strength: 5
- Charisma: 4
- Intelligence: 5
- Willpower: 6
- Essence: 3.85
- Reaction: 4

Skills
- Armed Combat: 7
- Athletics: 3
- Etiquette (Corporate): 4
- Etiquette (Street): 8
- Firearms: 5
- Interrogation: 5
- Leadership: 4
- Unarmed Combat: 5

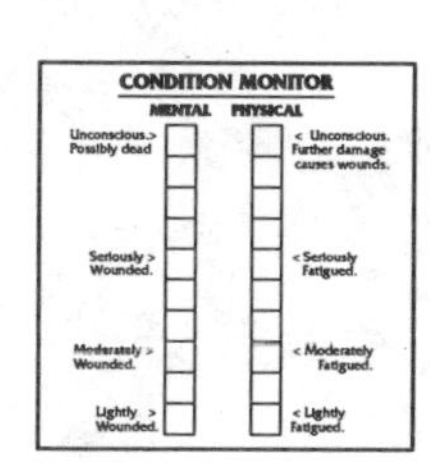

Special Skill
- Police Procedures: 6

Dice Pools
- Defense (Armed): 7
- Defense (Unarmed):5
- Dodge: 4

Cyberware
- Datajack
- Dermal Plating (2)
- Radio
- Retinal Modification: Flare Compensation

Gear
- 2 Concussion Grenades (4M3 Stun)
- Armor Jacket (5/3)
- Binoculars with Low-Light and Thermographic Imaging
- Katana [+1 Reach, 5M3]
- Ruger Super Warhawk [6 (Cylinder), 6 spare rounds, Laser Sight, 4M2]

BLACKWING

Blackwing is the essence of style and grace. An assassin for over ten years, he still loves every minute of it. Except for Cillian Nightprince, Blackwing's usual partner, the team with whom he is working on this mission is the best he has ever encountered. Blackwing is the leader of the group, but each one plays an important role on the team. No matter what the situation, Blackwing remains icy calm.

Blackwing wears only the most expensive clothes, favoring dark, solid colors and simple tailoring. His hair stays perfectly in place, no matter what the situation, and his smile is like a permanent fixture on his finely chiseled face.

Blackwing never seems to panic, keeping his cool during some of the most dangerous scrapes any assassin has ever encountered. Constantly alert to alternative actions and possibilities, he knows how to make the most of an enemy's mistake.

Blackwing will do whatever necessary to get the job done. He will protect his team if possible, making himself third priority. Blackwing is not afraid of dying, meaning he could attempt even the riskiest maneuvers.

Attributes
- Body: 5
- Quickness: 6
- Strength: 4
- Charisma: 3
- Intelligence: 5
- Willpower: 5
- Essence: .2
- Reaction: 5 (11)

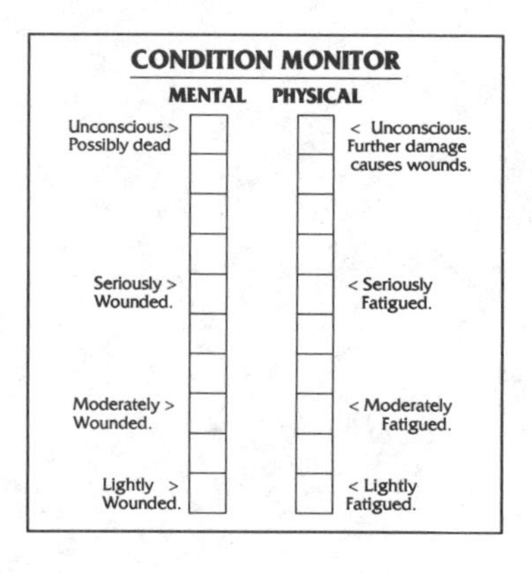
CONDITION MONITOR

MENTAL	PHYSICAL
Unconscious.> Possibly dead	< Unconscious. Further damage causes wounds.
Seriously > Wounded.	< Seriously Fatigued.
Moderately > Wounded.	< Moderately Fatigued.
Lightly > Wounded.	< Lightly Fatigued.

Skills
- Armed Combat: 5
- Car: 5
- Computer: 4
- Demolitions: 5
- Electronics: 4
- Etiquette (Street): 5
- Firearms: 8
- Unarmed Combat: 7

Dice Pools
- Defense (Armed): 5
- Defense (Unarmed): 7
- Dodge: 6

Cyberware
- Cyberears with Hearing Amplification
- Smartgun Link
- Wired Reflexes (3)

Gear:
- Ares Predator [10 (clip), 1 extra clip, Built-in Smartgun link, 4M2]
- DocWagon™ Contract (Gold)
- FN HAR [20 (clip), 2 extra clips, Built-in Smartgun link, Gas-Vent 2, 5M3]
- Tres Chic Armor Clothing (3/0)
- Eurocar Westwind 2000

Powers
- Low-Light Eyes

Weaknesses
- Allergy (Sunlight, Nuisance)

TUNDRA

Tundra is just beginning to wind down his career. He has been running the shadows for more years than he cares to remember, and the constant pressure is wearing him out. Having lived though some intense firefights, he is more than a little gun-shy. He will always lead with his biggest and best weapon, either spell or gun. If possible, he avoids hand-to-hand fighting. Like Blackwing, he knows this could well be his last mission and he is ready to die if necessary to complete it.

Attributes
- Body: 3 (4)
- Quickness: 4
- Strength: 4
- Charisma: 2
- Intelligence: 5
- Willpower: 5
- Essence: 5.2
- Magic: 5
- Reaction: 4 (6)

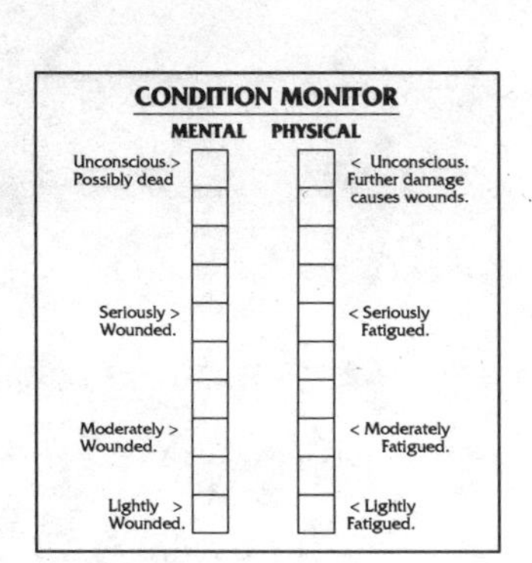

Skills
- Bike: 2
- Conjuring: 3
- Firearms: 4
- Magical Theory: 6
- Sorcery: 6
- Throwing Weapons: 3
- Unarmed Combat: 4

Dice Pools
- Astral: 16
- Defense (Armed): 1
- Defense (Unarmed): 4
- Dodge: 4
- Magic: 6

Cyberware
- Dermal Plating (1)
- Retractable Spurs (2M2)

Gear
- 2 Expendable Power Bolt Fetishes
- 2 Offensive Grenades (6M3)
- Armor Jacket (5/3)
- Armor Spell Lock (3 successes)
- Increase Reaction +2 Spell Lock
- Pocket Computer
- Uzi III SMG [16 (clip), 1 extra clip, Laser Sight, 4M3]
- Yamaha Rapier

Spells
- **Combat:**
  - Manaball: 5
  - Power Bolt: 5
- **Detection:**
  - Combat Sense: 4
  - Detect Enemies: 4
- **Health:**
  - Heal Severe Wounds: 4
  - Increase Reaction +2: 4
- **Manipulation:**
  - Armor: 4

Powers
- Low-Light Eyes

Weakness
- Allergy (Silver, Moderate)

HARPER

Harper is the new kid on the team. Blackwing and Tundra are the only people with whom she has ever worked and she treats them like family. She will do whatever she can to make sure they all come out of this safely. Harper, however, is not quite willing to die trying to get possession of the case. She would never run out on the others, but if they were obviously down and out, she would attempt to escape and seek revenge at a later date.

During combat, she will be the most magically active, often slipping into Astral Space to get a better view of her opponents. She excels at astral combat.

Attributes
- Body: 1
- Quickness: 4
- Strength: 1
- Charisma: 4
- Intelligence: 5
- Willpower: 5
- Essence: 6
- Magic: 6
- Reaction: 4

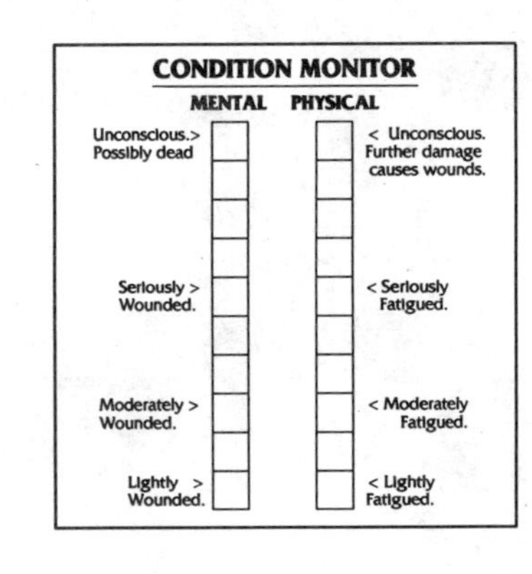

Skills
- Bike: 4
- Conjuring: 6
- Etiquette (Tribal): 4
- Firearms: 3
- Magical Theory: 6
- Sorcery: 7
- Unarmed Combat: 4

Dice Pools
- Astral: 18
- Defense (Armed): 1
- Defense (Unarmed): 4
- Dodge: 4
- Magic: 7

Gear
- 2 Antidote Patches (6)
- 2 Stimulant Patches (5)
- 3 Expendable Fetishes per Spell Known
- Armor Spell Lock (3 successes)
- Enfield AS7 Shotgun [10 (clip), 1 spare clip, Laser Sight, 4M3]
- Lined Coat (4/2)
- Pocket Computer
- Yamaha Rapier

Spells
- **Combat:**
  - Powerball: 4
  - Sleep: 6
- **Detection:**
  - Clairvoyance: 4
  - Mind Probe: 5
- **Health:**
  - Heal Moderate Wounds: 5
- **Illusion:**
  - Chaotic World: 5
- **Manipulation**
  - Magic Fingers: 4

Powers
- Low-Light Eyes

Weaknesses
- Allergy (Plastic, Mild)

ARLEESH

Arleesh is a Great Feathered Serpent. She has only been awake for the past ten months, making her feel still a bit out of things. She recently arrived in Seattle to do some slumming and learn more about modern Human culture. Shortly after arriving, she sensed the presence and activity of the idol and began to track it. As long as the idol remained within its barrier, however, she could make very little headway. Only when the object was free of its case could Arleesh begin to track it properly.

Though young for a Great Dragon, she is ancient compared to Geyswain. That means she has first-hand knowledge of the horrors associated with the power behind the idol. She will do everything within her power, including sacrificing her own life, to destroy it.

Arleesh is loyal only to herself, and she considers Humans little more than tools for accomplishing her own tasks. She has the integrity to keep her word to Humans, but she would lead them into Hell if that would further her mission.

In the statistics that follow, the number in parenthesis represents the value that applies to Arleesh when she is in Human form.

Attributes
- Body: 18 (8)
- Quickness: 6 x 2 (7)
- Strength: 40 (8)
- Charisma: 8
- Intelligence: 7
- Willpower: 12
- Essence: 12
- Magic: 12
- Reaction: 10 (7)

Dice Pools
- Astral: 34
- Defense (Armed): 5
- Defense (Unarmed): 8
- Dodge: 7
- Magic: 15

Skills
- Armed Combat: 6
- Athletics: 5
- Conjuring: 12
- Etiquette (Street): 4
- Interrogation: 8
- Leadership: 6
- Magical Theory: 12
- Negotiation: 5
- Psychology: 8
- Sorcery: 15
- Stealth: 5
- Throwing Weapons: 7
- Unarmed Combat: 8

Gear:
- 6 Shuriken (4L1)
- Medkit
- Mitsubishi Nightsky
- Orichalcum Sword [(3) +1 Reach, 8M2]
- Ruger Super Warhawk [6 (Cylinder), Laser Sight, 4M2]
- Trauma Patch (6)
- Tres Chic Armor Jacket (5/3)
- Wrist Computer, 50 Mp of memory

Spells

Combat:
- Fireball: 6
- Manaball: 10
- Power Bolt: 12
- Ram: 8
- Sleep: 10

Detection:
- Combat Sense: 7
- Detect Enemies: 8
- Mind Probe: 8

Health:
- Antidote Severe Toxin: 6
- Cure Moderate Disease: 6
- Heal Moderate Wounds: 8
- Increase Quickness +4: 6
- Increase Willpower +3: 5
- Treat Deadly Wounds: 5

Illusion:
- Chaotic World: 7
- Invisibility: 6
- Stink: 6

Manipulation:
- Armor: 9
- Barrier: 6
- Control Emotion: 8
- Hibernate: 10
- Petrify: 8
- Poltergeist: 8
- Turn to Goo: 8

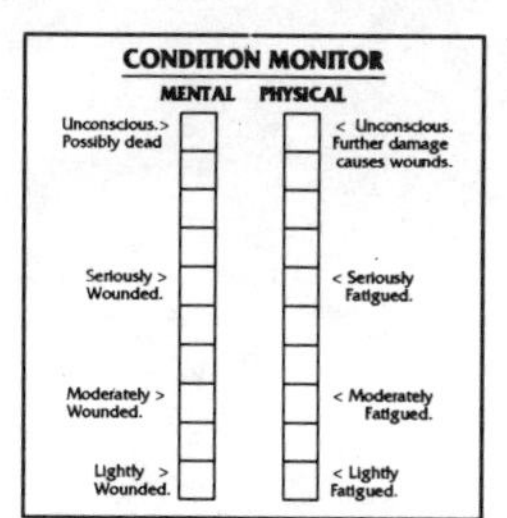

PICKING UP THE PIECES

AFTER THE ADVENTURE

It will take about a week or so before everything returns to normal and the runners' friends start talking to them again. Of course, no one will ever mention that there was any problem. It's all part of the biz, ya dig?

When the dust finally settles, Grissim could end up being a Contact, or at least an acquaintance, at Lone Star. He might just as easily become one of the runners' most hated adversaries. It all depends on how the runners treat Grissim or the other Lone Star troopers they encounter. If there's a long row of Lone Star bodies in the morgue, don't place any bets on Grissim being too friendly.

Bloodwing will get deported to Tir Tairngire. Who knows when he will return, or how upset he will be? Who knows if he will even survive his master's wrath at retrieving either an inert idol or none at all?

What happens to Arleesh is up to the gamemaster. She may never be heard from again, or she might someday return to lead the runners into more adventures. With friends like this, who needs fixers?

AWARDING KARMA

There's some opportunity for financial gain in this adventure, but not much. Karma, however, is plentiful.

TEAM KARMA

Divide up the following Karma Points among the surviving team members. In the fourth instance, where the idol is not destroyed, note that the minimum Karma Award should be 0.

No team members affected by the idol	3
Geyswain does not get idol	5
Idol destroyed	8
Idol not destroyed	-10

INDIVIDUAL KARMA

See page 160 of the **Shadowrun** basic rules.

PLAYING WITH DARKNESS

EXAMINING THE IDOL

Any magician should realize that the idol is an object of enormous power, no matter how mysterious or inexplicable. The gamemaster can use this realization as the means to keep the players from simply trying to toss the idol in the nearest dumpster once they start to find it a troublesome possession.

PHYSICAL EXAMINATION

The idol is just over 30 centimeters long and carved from deep-red stone. Its eyes are glowing and it holds a glowing pinkish ball to its chest. The object is vaguely demon-shaped and etched with symbols and patterns that have become faint and worn almost flat, either by the ravages of time or from handling. The object weighs a little more than two kilograms.

It is impossible to damage the idol in any way. The stone cannot be scratched, dented, chipped, or smashed. This also means that any scientific analysis requiring a chip, sample, or shard (even on a near-molecular level) is not possible. Any other method of analysis will produce only conflicting, inconclusive results.

Science be damned. This is real magic.

MAGICAL EXAMINATION

Beyond astral/assense investigation, the only possible magical examination of the idol is a scholarly one. A character with Magical Theory or a Hermetic Library can attempt to research the faint symbols and patterns still visible on the object, but with no conclusive results. Some of the design elements appear in documented magical symbology, but nothing can be definitively referenced.

ASTRAL EXAMINATION

Assensing the idol through Astral Perception will produce some useful information. The assensing character makes a Sorcery (12) Test to learn more.

ASSENSING THE IDOL

Successes	Result
0	The idol is magical.
1	Anyone with magical capabilities can use the idol as a Power Focus.
2	The idol has a Power Focus Rating of 12.
3	The object seems to tap into astral space for its power, as a normal focus, but something is odd about the way it does so.
4	The channels of the idol's power are oddly twisted. The paths seem to interlace normally with astral space, but then veer off at 90 degrees to another level of existence somewhere...
5+	It is from this "somewhere" that the idol draws its power.

Following any assensing die roll that produces 4 or more successes, the gamemaster should secretly make a Magic (6) Test for the assensing character. For the effects of failure or even the partial success of this test, see **Using The Idol,** below.

USING THE IDOL

Chances are one or more player characters will want to use the idol as a Power Focus. Let them; they are only digging their own graves.

AS A POWER FOCUS

As a Power Focus, the idol has a rating of 12. Any character with magical capabilities (a Magic Attribute 1 or higher) can use it, whether or not that character has spent Karma to bond the item. Though Power Focuses must normally be bonded to a specific user, any magician can use this idol as a Power Focus at any time.

Shamans who use the idol will suffer the same magical and physical effects as Hermetic mages, but they also suffer from the wrath of their totems. Shortly after first using the idol, the shaman's sleep is wracked by gruesome dreams of death, destruction, and decay. He sees the same horrifying images everywhere he turns during his waking hours, too, but it is as though the sights have been magnified one hundred times. The woman huddled in a doorway is no longer just a bag lady, but a wretched, diseased victim of corruption who is slowly being devoured by the physical and moral ills of the Sprawl. Asleep or awake, the shaman cannot escape these terrifying images.

If his Magic Attribute drops below half its original value, the shaman loses all his Totem bonuses or modifiers (whether or not he notices the loss). See **Effects Of The Idol,** below. Even if the shaman becomes free of the idol's influence because it has been removed or destroyed, he must conduct a ritual purge in his medicine lodge. The purge lasts a number of days equal to the number of points lost from his Magic Attribute, multiplied by 2. After the purge, he regains all his lost points. He only regains the points, however, if he completes the purging in a single block of time. Again, see **Effects Of The Idol**, below.

The idol functions exactly like any other Power Focus, except that it cannot, in any way, shape, or form, augment a Summoning. Any attempt is doomed to failure, though the player character will be unaware of why that is happening. As far as the player character is concerned, the Summoning is executed normally, but the gamemaster does not count the dice that using the idol as a Power Focus would normally contribute to the Magic Pool. If no successes are rolled, the summoned spirit will materialize, but in a twisted, corrupt form that will quickly break free from attempts to control it and go roaring off into the night. Any successes rolled result in the inexplicable failure of the Summoning, for no spirit comes through.

For Banishing, the idol can be used normally as a Power Focus.

If used in Ritual Magic, all involved in the ritual must make a Magic Test, per **Effects Of The Idol,** below.

EFFECTS OF THE IDOL

Anyone who attempts to use the idol's power opens himself up to great danger. Though using the idol may seem to produce some benefit, the source of the object's power is voracious. In exchange for the loan of its power, it demands and takes a piece of the user.

Whenever a character uses the idol as a Power Focus, he must make a Magic Test with a target number equal to the rating of the focus used. For example, if a magician decided to call up only 6 of the idol's 12 rating points, his Target Number for the Magic Test would be 6.

The gamemaster should make all the Magic Tests because the character involved is blind to the effect the idol is having on him, even if someone or something points out those effects in no uncertain terms.

After making the Magic Test, consult the table below.

MAGIC TEST

Successes	Result
0	The character suffers a Magic Attribute loss (see below) and a Major Physical Effect.
1	The character may suffer a Magic Attribute loss (see below) and a Minor Physical Effect.
2	The character suffers a Major Physical Effect (see below).
3	The character suffers a Minor Physical Effect (see below).
4	The character suffers no appreciable effect, except that the sensation of power is odd.
5+	The sensation that the character experiences when using the idol's power is so strange that it feels intrinsically wrong.

Magic Attribute Loss

If the Magic Test Table indicates that the character automatically suffers from a Magic Attribute loss, his Magic Attribute drops by 1 point, but he is unaware of it. He continues to operate as though the point had not been lost, and suffers no ill effects from the loss at this time. The gamemaster, who should be the only one aware of the loss, must keep track of the character's current actual Magic Attribute Rating.

If the Magic Test Table indicates a character might suffer a Magic Attribute loss, the gamemaster makes a secret Willpower Test against the same target used for the Magic Test. If there are any successes, the character suffers no loss of Magic Attribute points, but a Minor Physical Effect does occur. Failure indicates a loss of 1 point and a Minor Physical Effect.

Major Physical Effect

A Major Physical Effect affects a character's Attributes. To determine which Attribute suffers a Major Physical Effect, the gamemaster rolls 1D6 and consults the table below. In each case, the character loses1 rating point from the Attribute, down to a minimum value of 1.

ATTRIBUTE LOSS

1D6	Attribute
1 – 2	Body
3 – 4	Quickness
5 – 6	Strength

At this point, the gamemaster must take the affected player aside to inform him of this Attribute loss. He also tells the player that his *character* views his current physical condition as *normal* and that no amount of argument from the other runners can persuade him that something is wrong. The player should roleplay the loss, but not focus on it. If the other player characters notice the effect, so be it.

The Attribute loss should also have some physical manifestation similar to those suggested for a Minor Physical Effect, below. This could be a sudden weight loss for Body, slight hand tremors for Quickness, or a general feeling of weakness for Strength. If prolonged use of the idol causes continued Attribute loss, the effects should grow increasingly more pronounced.

Minor Physical Effect

Unlike a Major Physical Effect, the Minor Effect has no effect on the character in any other area beyond roleplaying. The gamemaster decides the nature of the Minor Effect, but it should be appropriate to the character involved. Some possibilities:

- A lock of hair turns white.
- A change in eye color.
- Developing a nervous twitch or tick.
- Non-sentient animals, or those with empathic abilities, seem frightened of the character.
- A sudden personality change.
- A change in the way the character casts a spell.
- A change in tone or pitch of voice.
- A speed-up or slow-down in metabolism, requiring more or less food.
- Needing more or less sleep.
- Developing an allergy, similar to those of Metahumans.

Again, the gamemaster informs the affected player, but the character still considers himself to be perfectly normal. The player should roleplay the Physical Effect, but without accenting it so much that it becomes the focus of his character.

BREAKING THE INFLUENCE

There are three ways to break the influence of the idol, the first two require doing something to the idol and are none too pleasant for the influenced character. The third method calls for the influenced character to accomplish a Herculean effort of will.

An influenced character immediately suffers devastating effects anytime he is separated from the idol by a distance greater than a number of meters equal to his Willpower. First, his Magic Attribute drops to the value the gamemaster has recorded, and all his Dice Pools are adjusted to reflect this. He is also immediately subjected to 1D6 Major Physical Effects, but a single success in a Willpower (12) Test will neutralize each Effect. He also immediately suffers a Resisted 6D1 Stun attack that can be staged down using Body dice rolled against a Target Number 12. Returning the idol to the character will not reverse any physical effects the character has suffered, but his Magic Attribute returns to its original level.

If the idol should be destroyed, the character suffers the same effects described above.

Whether the character has suffered Physical Effects because of prolonged separation from the idol or because of its destruction, the character's Attributes, including Magic, gradually return to normal, at a rate of 1 point per 24 hours. No amount of magic or medical attention will alter that rate. During this time, the character experiences constant nightmares and hallucinations similar to withdrawal from serious addiction to any powerful drug. The visions will be of death and decay, but will slowly begin to fade.

If the player wishes, he may keep whatever Minor Effect his character suffered.

The third method of breaking the idol's influence only occurs when the character's Magic Attribute is about to drop to 0. At that time, the player must make a Willpower (24) test. If he rolls one success, he suddenly realizes what has been happening to him and throws off the idol's influence. He will gradually, as indicated above, regain any lost Attribute Points as long as he does not use the idol's power again. If he does, he must make a final Willpower Test to save his soul.

If the character fails the roll, there is still time, but the matter is out of his hands. He will become gradually aware of a falling sensation, as though he were sliding down a muddy embankment into a dark, unfathomable pool. This will happen over a period of days equal to his Willpower Attribute Rating. If the idol can be separated from him or destroyed within that period of time, the character can be saved, as above. If not, the character goes irrevocably insane at the end of the designated time period. In his last coherent moments, he experiences an overwhelming horror as the secrets of the idol's power are revealed to him.

DESIRE FOR THE IDOL

Once any influenced character's Magic Attribute falls below half its original rating, he begins to experience a deep urge to keep and use the idol, and certainly will not let it be taken from him, much less destroyed.

As before, the gamemaster discusses this roleplaying aspect of the idol's influence with the affected player before implementation.

Lone Star quiet on Lochlann massacre

TACOMA—Authorities from Lone Star Security are still refusing to comment on reports of a major disaster occurring last night at the Lochlann Center in downtown Tacoma. An unconfirmed source said that at least 150 employees of the real estate firm were found dead this morning by Lone Star guards responding to an anonymous tip.

Preliminary reports are listing the cause of death as being "magically induced." The source goes on to say, however, that Lone Star forensic experts are at a loss to identify the exact nature of the magic involved.

Jacob Bright, corporate spokesperson for Lone Star Security, refused to answer any questions regarding Lochlann, saying only that an "incident" had occurred at the facility and was currently under investigation. Bright would neither confirm nor deny claims that Geyswain, the Western Dragon who is Lochlann's founder and CEO, was among those found dead.

As of five o'clock this morning, armed Lone Star forces remained at Lochlann, sealing off the entire building and preventing anyone from entering.

Said one employee not on duty yesterday, "We're just a real estate company. This kind of thing doesn't happen here. At least that's what I always thought."

Brotherhood moves uptown

A spokesperson for the Universal Brotherhood told reporters today that the organization would be opening awareness centers in downtown Seattle and Tacoma by summer.

Niles Patrick indicated that these facilities would follow closely the style of numerous centers already in operation throughout low-income neighborhoods. "It isn't only the poor and unaccomplished who need emotional and psychological support," said Patrick. "Our studies have shown that executives at all levels are leading miserable, unfulfilled lives without ever realizing there is someting they can do about it. Participation in our programs will put them on the path of self-determination and achievement."

Support for the actions of the Universal Brotherhood appear to be growing at the neighborhood level. Still, some city leaders have accused the organization of being nothing more than a front for anti-establishment sentiment.

"How can they possibly say that?" asked Patrick when told of the accusation. "Our only purpose is to raise an individual's personal awareness so that he or she can become a reasoning, understanding citizen aware of his place in the universe."

Judge named to crime panel

Appellate court justice Evan Gooch was named to the Seattle Crime Commission Select Panel on Containment, it was announced yesterday.

Justice Gooch fills one of two remaining spaces on the panel formed by Governor Schultz to investigate preventive measures against crime.

Gooch, known as "Hanging Evan" for his stiff sentencing practices, said he brings "Twenty-three years of facing miscerants" to the panel. Gooch began his career as a prosecutor, becoming an associate judge 12 years ago. He was appointed to the appellate bench five years ago.

Among Gooch's most memorable achievements were the prosecution of the surviving Screamin' Meemies, the first Ork gang eradicated by the Gang Task Force; and his presiding over the year-long trial of organized crime leader Hano Tomas, who was sentenced to serve 24 consecutive life sentences.

Seek info in hit-and-run

Seattle Police are at a loss in their investigation of a hit-and-run accident last Thursday.

Seven-year-old Tamsin Douglas-Kinsal was run over by a motorcyclist Thursday afternoon around 3 pm. She was struck at 6th Ave. South and Main Street, just after leaving Kobe Terrace Park with her aunt, Madigan Kinsal.

Ms. Kinsal, who was slightly injured, said two bikers were speeding north on 6th, with pedestrians scrambling to get out of their way. Kinsal says Tamsin slipped as her aunt tried to pull her out of the bikes' path, and the biker "just ran right over her", yelling something unintelligible.

Kinsal reported that both bikers were wearing similar gaudy clothing, leading police to assume they are members of a go-gang. Kinsal has been unable to positively identify the gang clothing after examining police photos.

Meanwhile, police have been unable to find any witnesses to the incident. People questioned on the scene maintain that they "didn't see a thing" or that "it happened too fast" to make any identification.

Police Lieutenant Avery Milkuski, head of the investigation, says that fear of gang retaliation has probably kept witnesses from being more forthcoming. "It is ridiculous that nobody would notice noisy, speeding bikers at a crowded downtown intersection in broad daylight," Milkuski said.

Milkuski says that the police will offer full protection to anyone who comes forward with information about the accident.

The victim's family has offered a reward of 5000¥ for useful information. One family member said they may hire private investigators. "The police are doing what they can, but they are too busy to spend the time tracking down information. This is just another case to them, but it's our little Tamsin."

Private services were held for the girl Monday.

Brighton, Euphoria release new sims

In an obvious move to regain the entertainment spotlight, both MegaMedia and Brilliant Genesis have rushed releases of new sims by their respective mega-stars, Honey Brighton and Euphoria. The Euphoria sim, *Final Fling,* is her first without co-star Hans Vandenburg. MegaMedia continues to deny rumors that a falling-out between Euphoria and Vandenburg is the reason for her solo effort. Company sources say it is simply an effort to allow Euphoria to shine on her own.

The Brighton sim *Rock Solid* is the controversial project Brighton and producer/director Witt Lipton took with them last year when they defected from MegaMedia. That defection rocked the entertainment industry and started an avalanche of lawsuits that have yet to be settled. The release of *Rock Solid* is expected to be the biggest saturation release from Brilliant Genesis to date.

Krasnow named city editor

Bruce Krasnow II will assume duties as News-Intelligencer city editor February 1, publisher Louise Berns announced Friday.

Krasnow replaces George Harmon, who is retiring to a retreat in Salish. Harmon, the first Elf reporter at the News-Intelligencer, was known for his evenhanded coverage of both Metahuman and Human concerns.

Krasnow has been a city reporter with the News-Intelligencer for six years, and has earned a reputation for his investigative reports. His series on building permit and inspection irregularities, "Higher, Faster, Weaker," won a North American Press award in 2048.

Krasnow pledges the News-Intelligencer city pages will remain "committed to serving this city and its citizens by celebrating the good and exposing the bad."

Chips recalled

MindTrips, a CAS-based chip manufacturer, has issued a recall order for simsense chips in its "Tourist Log" line.

The chips are *Visiting Scenic Japan* and *Visiting the Hills of Thailand*, stock numbers BV-JR32-1897 and BV-TM34-1884 respectively, and come in a yellow and green package

Dozens of customers have reported extreme headaches after using the chips, a company spokesperson said. Two were hospitalized with temporary blindness, but have recovered fully.

The spokesperson said that programming bugs had been introduced while updating chips for new cyberimplants. The chips are supposed to be compatible with older versions of the hardware, but are apparently producing "neural feedback" in some users.

Consumers who have purchased these chips, or any MindTrips chips they suspect may be incompatible with their hardware, may bring the chips to any MindTrips dealer, or return them to the corporation for a full refund.

Sewage complaints disrupt meeting

A city planning meeting was disrupted by angry residents demanding immediate sewer repairs in the Des Moines neighborhood.

Residents stood on chairs and tables, waving signs and chanting "Clean it up!" and "Water, water everywhere, and every drop does stink!"

Clayton Lucas, speaking for the Des Moines Residents Association, said that the sewers have been backed up for a month, creating "first an unsightly nuisance, now a major health hazard, soon to be a major political issue."

Lucas, on behalf of the neighbors, demanded immediate sewer work, threatening to disrupt construction at two city building sites, and even to disrupt the spring festival, saying "no money for luxuries while we're living in [fecal matter]."

City Commissioner Kenneth Keenan said the city is fully aware of the issue, and plans cleanup as soon as heavy equipment is available.

Squatters fire in lux neighborhood kills 3

At least three persons were killed Tuesday by a fire in an officially empty building in the luxurious Alki neighborhood in downtown Seattle.

The deserted three-story retail/office structure was home to over a dozen squatters, fire investigators said. The transient nature of the occupants, and their illegal status, makes positive identification of the dead difficult.

Neighbors said they had complained numerous times to police and security squads about the squatters in the building, and did not understand why they were still there.

The building was gutted, with only one partial wall still standing. Fire marshalls were unable to give a cause for the blaze.

Regular occupants of the building report two persons unaccounted for who do not match the corpses found. A fire department member said the rubble will not be searched for more bodies. The one wall still standing presents a danger to searchers, and there are no guarantees that the missing were in the building at the time.

Two of the dead have been tentatively identified as Birdie McGee, a woman in her late 40s, and a male dwarf, about 30, known only as Shamus. The third corpse is either an Elf or Human male, 1.9m tall, probably between 19-35 years old. Both the female and the unidentified male bodies showed signs of violence.

Squatters report as missing a female Dwarf about 30, known as Gemma, the companion of Shamus; and a male Human in his early twenties called Freddie the Lip. One reported Freddie's actual last name as either Sherman or Sheridan.

If the players are unsuccessful, give them this to read

Seattle News-Intelligencer Update-Net January 15/14:00/Local Seattle Stories

Strange fire destroys Lochlann

TACOMA—Authorities from Lone Star Security spent the day sifting through the rubble of the Lochlann Center, hoping to find any clues to the cause of last night's fire that gutted the building, killing at least 150 employees.

While no explanations have yet been firmly established, early reports from Lone Star indicate that the destruction of the real estate and investment company may have been "magically induced." Various sightings were made of heavy astral activity in and around Lochlann just prior to the fire.

Jacob Bright, corporate spokesperson for Lone Star Security, reported that a full investigation was currently underway, and would look into these sightings. Bright also confirmed that the body of an unidentified, unusually large feathered serpent was found amongst the ruins.

As of this morning, there had been no official reaction from Lochlann Center's founder and CEO, Geyswain. In fact, the Western Dragon Geyswain has not been seen in public since before the disaster occurred.

Meanwhile, the search for more information continues. Said one Lochlann employee not on duty yesterday, "We're just a real estate company. This kind of thing doesn't happen here. At least that's what I always thought."

Brotherhood moves uptown

A spokesperson for the Universal Brotherhood told reporters today that the organization would be opening awareness centers in downtown Seattle and Tacoma by summer.

Niles Patrick indicated that these facilities would follow closely the style of numerous centers already in operation throughout low-income neighborhoods. "It isn't only the poor and unaccomplished who need emotional and psychological support," said Patrick. "Our studies have shown that executives at all levels are leading miserable, unfulfilled lives without ever realizing there is someting they can do about it. Participation in our programs will put them on the path of self-determination and achievement."

Support for the actions of the Universal Brotherhood appear to be growing at the neighborhood level. Still, some city leaders have accused the organization of being nothing more than a front for anti-establishment sentiment.

"How can they possibly say that?" asked Patrick when told of the accusation. "Our only purpose is to raise an individual's personal awareness so that he or she can become a reasoning, understanding citizen aware of his place in the universe."

Judge named to crime panel

Appellate court justice Evan Gooch was named to the Seattle Crime Commission Select Panel on Containment, it was announced yesterday.

Justice Gooch fills one of two remaining spaces on the panel formed by Governor Schultz to investigate preventive measures against crime.

Gooch, known as "Hanging Evan" for his stiff sentencing practices, said he brings "Twenty-three years of facing miscerants" to the panel. Gooch began his career as a prosecutor, becoming an associate judge 12 years ago. He was appointed to the appellate bench five years ago.

Among Gooch's most memorable achievements were the prosecution of the surviving Screamin' Meemies, the first Ork gang eradicated by the Gang Task Force; and his presiding over the year-long trial of organized crime leader Hano Tomas, who was sentenced to serve 24 consecutive life sentences.

Seek info in hit-and-run

Seattle Police are at a loss in their investigation of a hit-and-run accident last Thursday.

Seven-year-old Tamsin Douglas-Kinsal was run over by a motorcyclist Thursday afternoon around 3 pm. She was struck at 6th Ave. South and Main Street, just after leaving Kobe Terrace Park with her aunt, Madigan Kinsal.

Ms. Kinsal, who was slightly injured, said two bikers were speeding north on 6th, with pedestrians scrambling to get out of their way. Kinsal says Tamsin slipped as her aunt tried to pull her out of the bikes' path, and the biker "just ran right over her", yelling something unintelligible.

Kinsal reported that both bikers were wearing similar gaudy clothing, leading police to assume they are members of a go-gang. Kinsal has been unable to positively identify the gang clothing after examining police photos.

Meanwhile, police have been unable to find any witnesses to the incident. People questioned on the scene maintain that they "didn't see a thing" or that "it happened too fast" to make any identification.

Police Lieutenant Avery Milkuski, head of the investigation, says that fear of gang retaliation has probably kept witnesses from being more forthcoming. "It is ridiculous that nobody would notice noisy, speeding bikers at a crowded downtown intersection in broad daylight," Milkuski said.

Milkuski says that the police will offer full protection to anyone who comes forward with information about the accident.

The victim's family has offered a reward of 5000¥ for useful information. One family member said they may hire private investigators. "The police are doing what they can, but they are too busy to spend the time tracking down information. This is just another case to them, but it's our little Tamsin."

Private services were held for the girl Monday.

Go 1: Local News / 2: World News / 3: Sports News / 4: Weather Update / 5: Business Report / 6: Lifestyle features / 7: Entertainment

Brighton, Euphoria release new sims

In an obvious move to regain the entertainment spotlight, both MegaMedia and Brilliant Genesis have rushed releases of new sims by their respective mega-stars, Honey Brighton and Euphoria. The Euphoria sim, *Final Fling,* is her first without co-star Hans Vandenburg. MegaMedia continues to deny rumors that a falling-out between Euphoria and Vandenburg is the reason for her solo effort. Company sources say it is simply an effort to allow Euphoria to shine on her own.

The Brighton sim *Rock Solid* is the controversial project Brighton and producer/director Witt Lipton took with them last year when they defected from MegaMedia. That defection rocked the entertainment industry and started an avalanche of lawsuits that have yet to be settled. The release of *Rock Solid* is expected to be the biggest saturation release from Brilliant Genesis to date.

Chips recalled

MindTrips, a CAS-based chip manufacturer, has issued a recall order for simsense chips in its "Tourist Log" line.

The chips are *Visiting Scenic Japan* and *Visiting the Hills of Thailand*, stock numbers BV-JR32-1897 and BV-TM34-1884 respectively, and come in a yellow and green package

Dozens of customers have reported extreme headaches after using the chips, a company spokesperson said. Two were hospitalized with temporary blindness, but have recovered fully.

The spokesperson said that programming bugs had been introduced while updating chips for new cyberimplants. The chips are supposed to be compatible with older versions of the hardware, but are apparently producing "neural feedback" in some users.

Consumers who have purchased these chips, or any MindTrips chips they suspect may be incompatible with their hardware, may bring the chips to any MindTrips dealer, or return them to the corporation for a full refund.

Sewage complaints disrupt meeting

A city planning meeting was disrupted by angry residents demanding immediate sewer repairs in the Des Moines neighborhood.

Residents stood on chairs and tables, waving signs and chanting "Clean it up!" and "Water, water everywhere, and every drop does stink!"

Clayton Lucas, speaking for the Des Moines Residents Association, said that the sewers have been backed up for a month, creating "first an unsightly nuisance, now a major health hazard, soon to be a major political issue."

Lucas, on behalf of the neighbors, demanded immediate sewer work, threatening to disrupt construction at two city building sites, and even to disrupt the spring festival, saying "no money for luxuries while we're living in [fecal matter]."

City Commissioner Kenneth Keenan said the city is fully aware of the issue, and plans cleanup as soon as heavy equipment is available.

Krasnow named city editor

Bruce Krasnow II will assume duties as News-Intelligencer city editor February 1, publisher Louise Berns announced Friday.

Krasnow replaces George Harmon, who is retiring to a retreat in Salish. Harmon, the first Elf reporter at the News-Intelligencer, was known for his evenhanded coverage of both Metahuman and Human concerns.

Krasnow has been a city reporter with the News-Intelligencer for six years, and has earned a reputation for his investigative reports. His series on building permit and inspection irregularities, "Higher, Faster, Weaker," won a North American Press award in 2048.

Krasnow pledges the News-Intelligencer city pages will remain "committed to serving this city and its citizens by celebrating the good and exposing the bad."

Squatters fire in lux neighborhood kills 3

At least three persons were killed Tuesday by a fire in an officially empty building in the luxurious Alki neighborhood in downtown Seattle.

The deserted three-story retail/office structure was home to over a dozen squatters, fire investigators said. The transient nature of the occupants, and their illegal status, makes positive identification of the dead difficult.

Neighbors said they had complained numerous times to police and security squads about the squatters in the building, and did not understand why they were still there.

The building was gutted, with only one partial wall still standing. Fire marshalls were unable to give a cause for the blaze.

Regular occupants of the building report two persons unaccounted for who do not match the corpses found. A fire department member said the rubble will not be searched for more bodies. The one wall still standing presents a danger to searchers, and there are no guarantees that the missing were in the building at the time.

Two of the dead have been tentatively identified as Birdie McGee, a woman in her late 40s, and a male dwarf, about 30, known only as Shamus. The third corpse is either an Elf or Human male, 1.9m tall, probably between 19-35 years old. Both the female and the unidentified male bodies showed signs of violence.

Squatters report as missing a female Dwarf about 30, known as Gemma, the companion of Shamus; and a male Human in his early twenties called Freddie the Lip. One reported Freddie's actual last name as either Sherman or Sheridan.

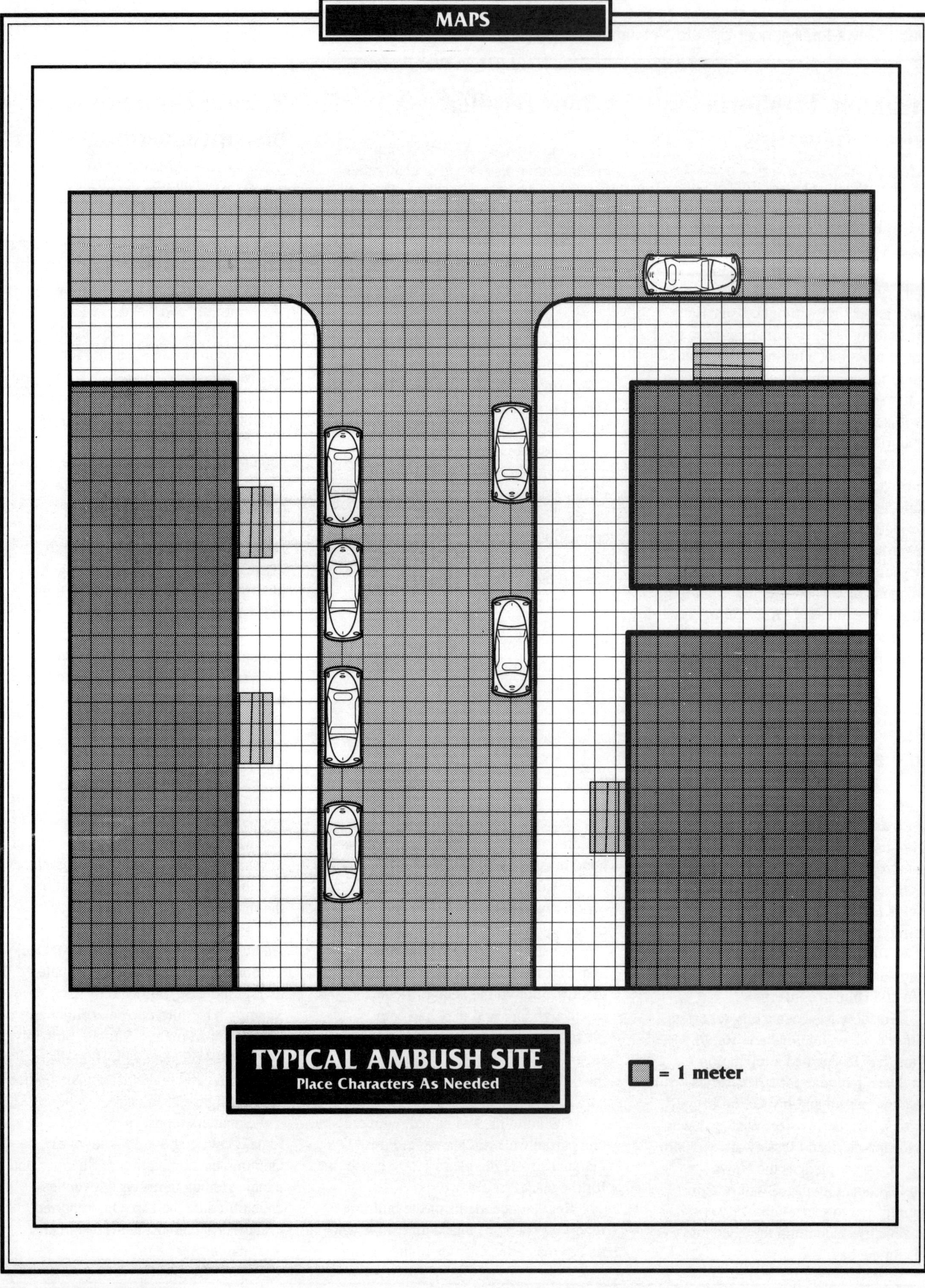
TYPICAL AMBUSH SITE
Place Characters As Needed
= 1 meter

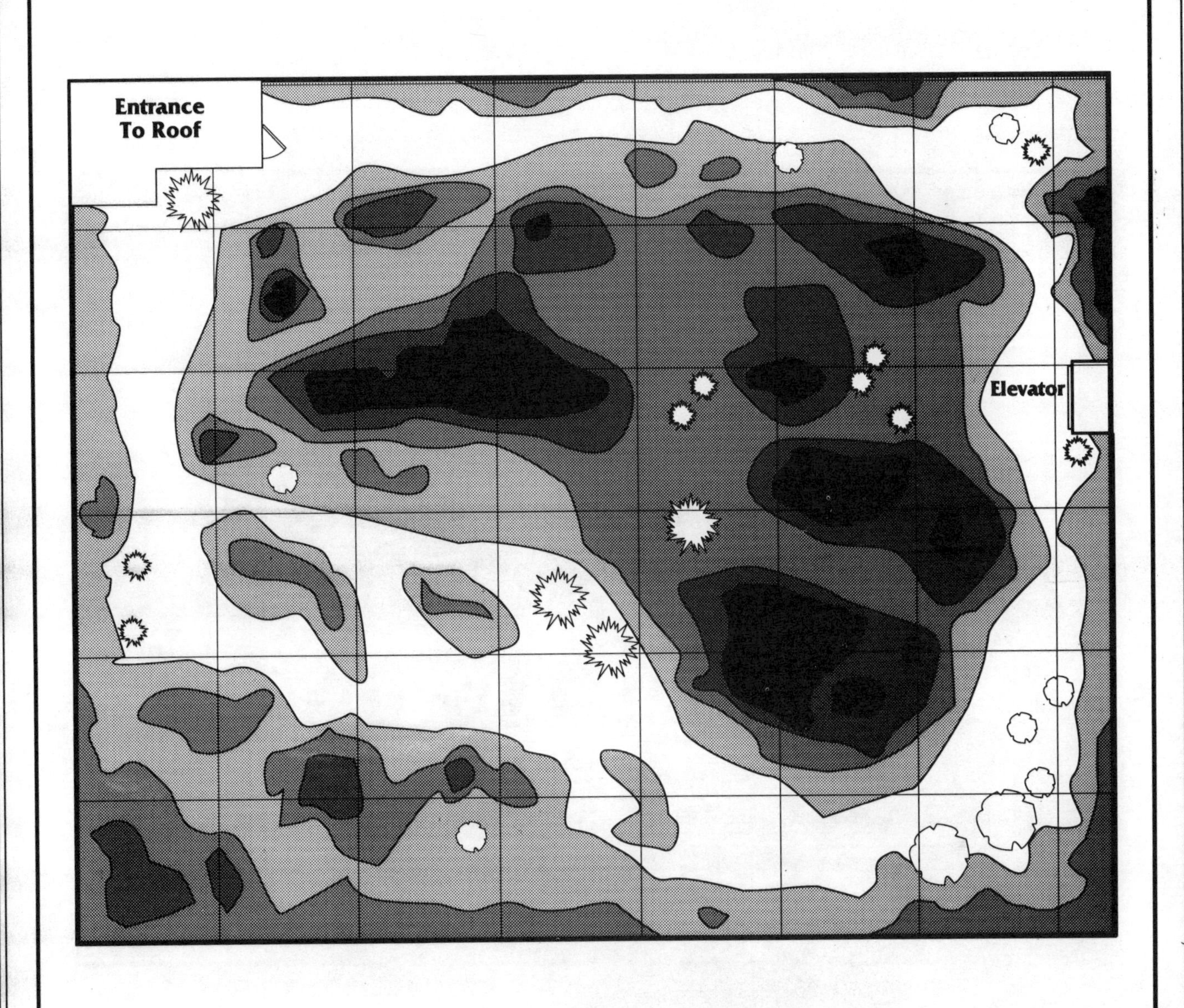

 = 75 meters

 = 2 meters high

 = 4 meters high

 = 6 meters high

 = 8 meters high

 = 10 meters high

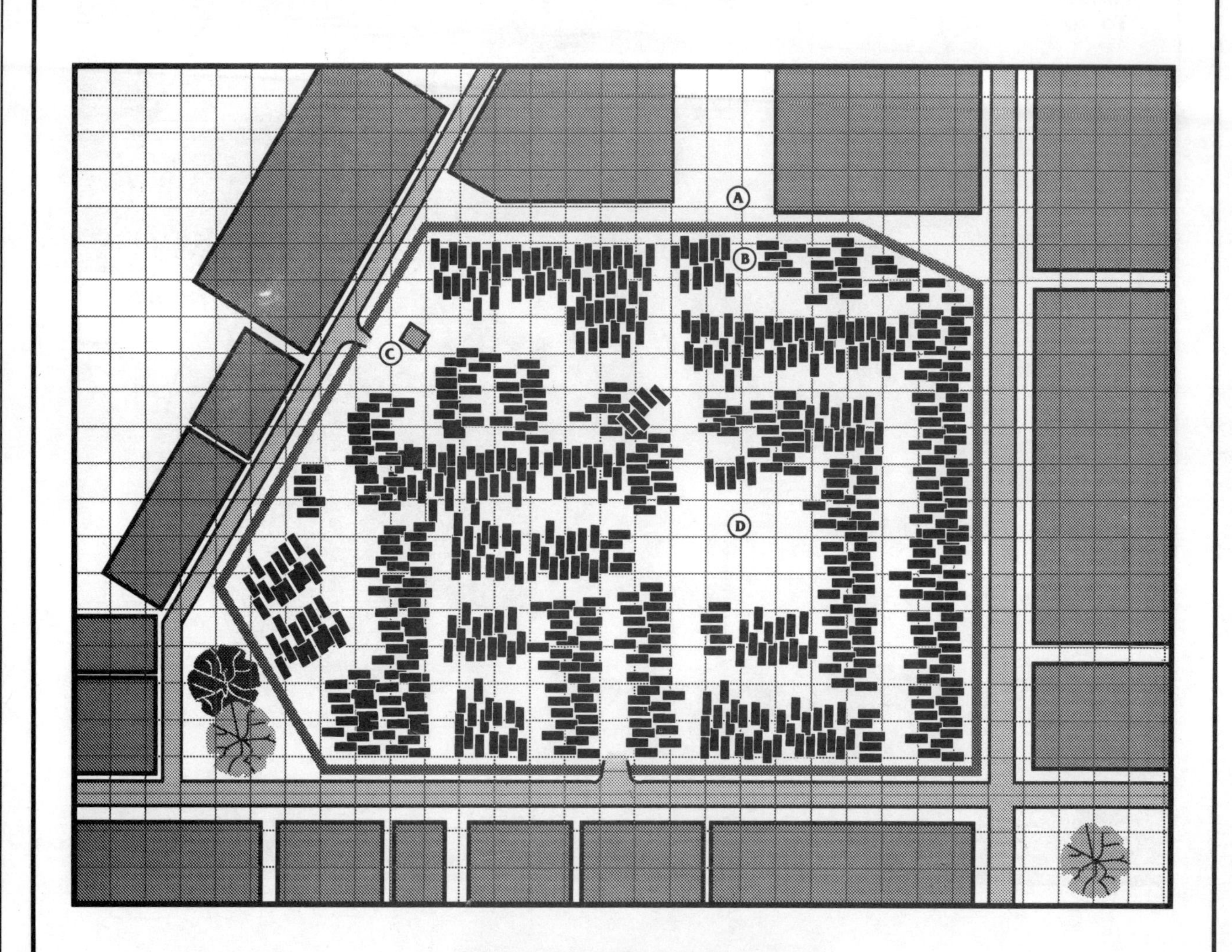

Black's Junk Yard

A = Tunnel Entrance
B = Tunnel Exit
C = Citymaster Entrance
D = Meeting Place

= 5 meters

= wrecked cars

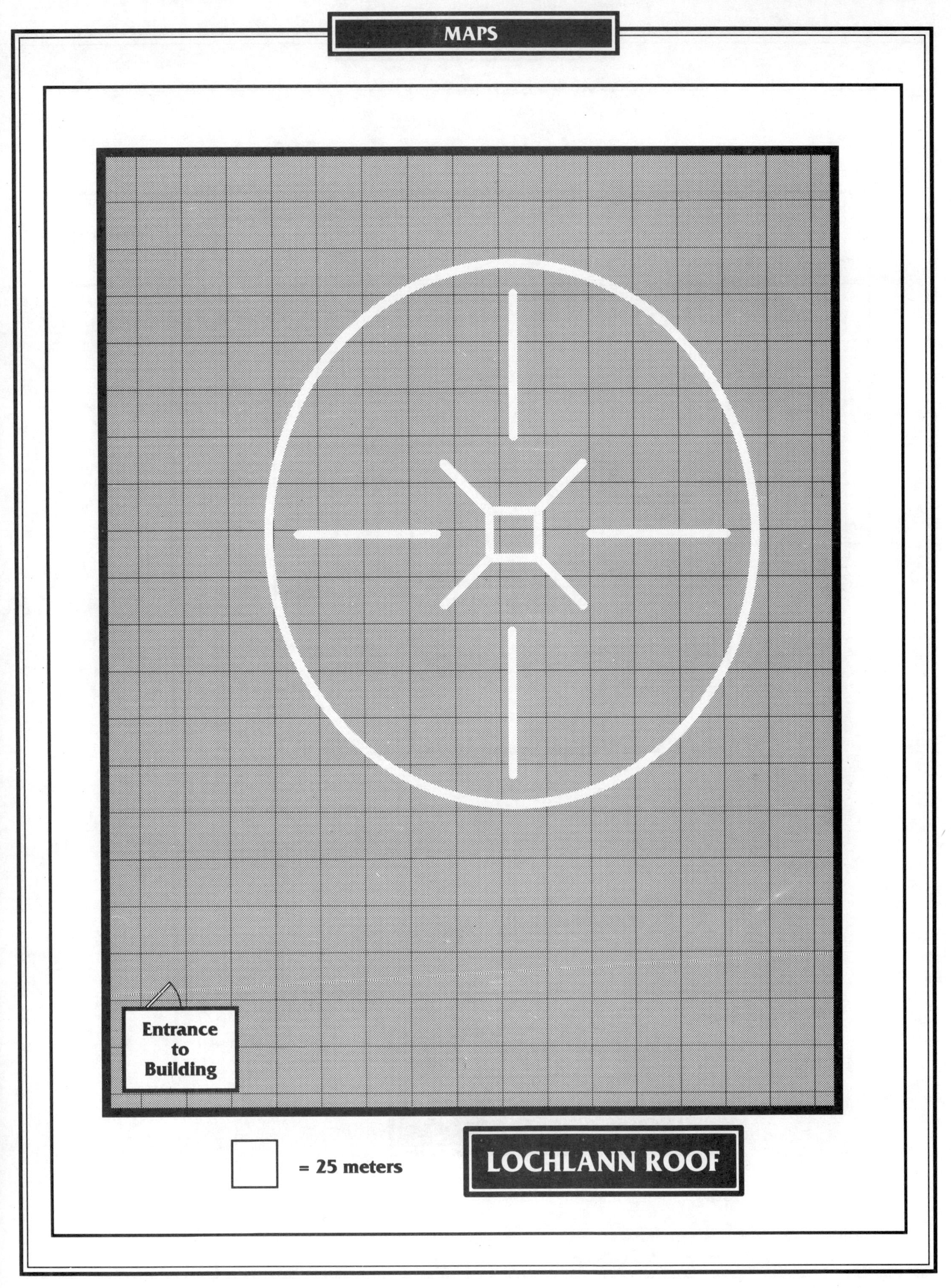
Entrance
to
Building
= 25 meters
LOCHLANN ROOF

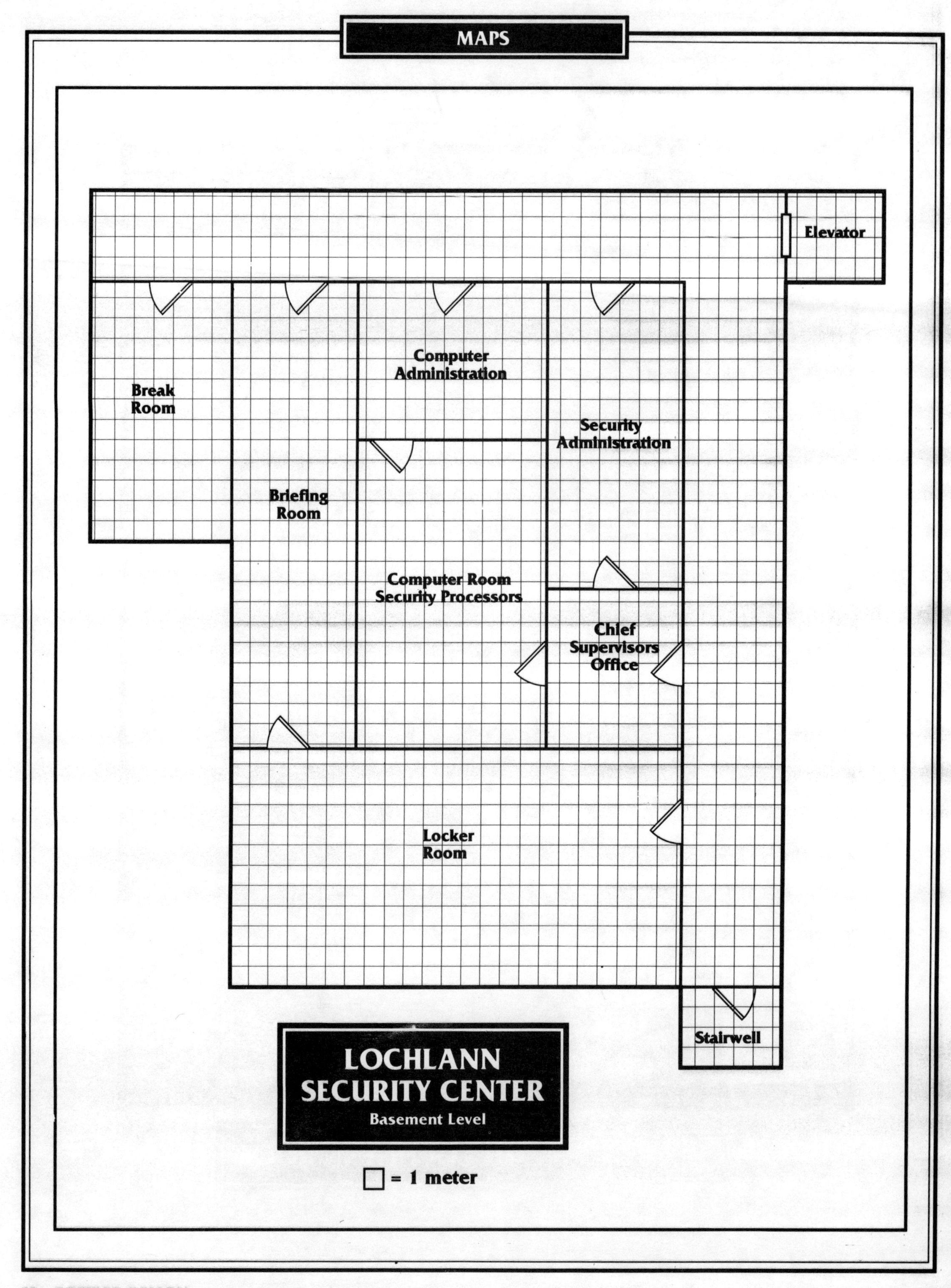
Elevator
Break Room
Computer Administration
Security Administration
Briefing Room
Computer Room Security Processors
Chief Supervisors Office
Locker Room
Stairwell
LOCHLANN SECURITY CENTER
Basement Level
= 1 meter